ADVOCACY
IN COURT

ADVOCACY IN COURT

A Beginner's Guide

Written by

Keith Evans

MA (Cantab), of the Middle Temple and Gray's Inn,
Barrister, Attorney of the State of California

With illustrations by the author

BLACKSTONE
PRESS LIMITED

Published in Great Britain 1995 by Blackstone Press Limited,
9–15 Aldine Street, London W12 8AW. Telephone: 0181-740 1173

First edition 1983
Reprinted 1983, 1985, 1992
Second edition 1995

ISBN: 1 85431 458 0

Typeset by Style Photosetting Ltd, Mayfield, East Sussex
Printed by Livesey Ltd, Shrewsbury, Shropshire

Contents

For Lisa, Kit and Zoë

Preface

There have been immense changes in the law and in the legal professions of England and Wales since this book was first published in the early 1980s. Indeed, its original title — Advocacy *at the Bar* — a Beginner's Guide — is now completely obsolete. In the early 1990s there came about a change which would have been unthinkable even twenty years earlier. Solicitors acquired the right to appear as advocates in every court in the Kingdom. This swept away the barristers' centuries-long 'exclusive right of audience' in the higher courts, and caused some people to fear for the continued existence of the Bar.

Where it is likely to lead is impossible to tell. Certainly, it is a seven-league step towards fusion of the two separate professions, though whether there will in fact be fusion is anybody's guess. It's somewhat ironic, indeed, that this should have happened when it did. For across the Atlantic, in the United States, there is an ever-strengthening body of opinion that wants to split the American Bar into specialist trial-lawyers and the rest.

Appearing as an advocate in court is the most challenging thing a lawyer can do: it is the sharp end of lawyering and it calls not only for courage but a great deal of skill as well. Most advocates would agree that it usually takes several years of experience to be truly competent, and, as many magistrates and jurors could attest, some lawyers never rise to that basic standard. For centuries there has been precious little teaching available for the newcomer and we have had to muddle through the learning process as best we could. But things are different now, and far from being about to watch a fall-off in the standards of British advocacy as a result of solicitor-advocates coming into the higher courts, we may well be about to witness a general raising of standards all round.

There are two good reasons for such optimism. First, the solicitor-advocate has to acquire what is effectively a *licence* to appear in the higher courts. Because of this the Law Society is organising the formal teaching of advocacy, the drawing up of codes of behaviour and a listing of those things an advocate really should know before setting foot in court. Most would-be solicitor-advocates are going to receive more formal training than most senior members of the Bar ever received themselves. One hopes the Law Society will make sure their advocacy training is top-notch, and that this great opportunity for setting new standards will not be missed.

The second reason for optimism is the barristers' response to the challenges of the times. They, too, are organising the much-more-formal teaching of advocacy. Middle Temple, for example, under the leadership of Michael Sherrard QC, is creating a training scheme which promises to be second to none. One of the finest advocates of his day, Master Sherrard is harnessing the skills and experience of other outstanding advocates so that the young Middle Templar will get an astonishingly high standard of instruction. If this works out as well as it could, the results should be exciting.

For Britain needs a cadre of competent, skilled, courageous advocates now, more urgently than at any time during the last two hundred years or so. A weak, divided government, more unpopular with the electorate than any within living memory, has enacted laws which have changed the face of British justice. The *right of silence* has been abolished. Under the terrible pressures caused by the 'troubles' in Ireland, the right of the accused to remain silent was whittled away, both by legislature and bench, and, now, this diminishment in the rights of the citizen has been extended to the whole of Great Britain. It is ironic that, so many centuries after Cromwell, the troubles of Ireland should have dealt such a body blow to British justice, for it was in Ireland, in the year 1790, that John Curran spoke those famous words about Liberty:

> The condition upon which God hath given liberty to man is *eternal vigilance;* which condition if he break, servitude is at once the consequence of his crime, and the punishment of his guilt.

Eternal vigilance has worn a bit thin in today's Britain, and with the right of silence gone, and the burden of proof in criminal cases having been reduced to a *prima facie* case bolstered by the accused's failure to explain himself, we have come a long way from the days when Devlin J was able to direct the jury:

> . . . he stood on his rights and did not speak. I have made it quite clear that I am not criticising that. I do not criticise it at all, and I hope the day will never come when the right is denied to any Englishman. The law on this matter reflects the natural voice of England and it always has — our horror at the idea that a man may be questioned and forced to speak and perhaps forced to condemn himself out of his own mouth. We afford to everyone at the beginning and at every stage and to the very end the right to say: Ask me no questions. I shall answer none. Prove your case!

It has been a remarkable fifty years, indeed, in the history of British justice. If you are resolved to be an advocate, it is important for you to be aware of those changes. If you can find the time and energy to ferret out and understand how those changes came about so much the better. One of the biggest of them was the abandonment of the civil jury. Go and read *any* legal memoirs concerning the courts before World War II and you realise that trial by jury always used to be the *norm* — in the county court as well as high court. Now it is trial by judge alone in virtually all civil disputes — the only exceptions are defamation, false imprisonment and malicious prosecution. It is an illustration of the way the Executive, unless prevented, cuts back on freedoms that it regards as inconvenient or hampering. The right to challenge jurors went the same way.

Although the right of silence was abolished only in 1994 in England and Wales, there is already a body of case law on the subject. These cases come out of Northern Ireland, where the accused's right of silence disappeared in 1988, and there is at least one directly relevant decision by the House of Lords. In *Kevin Murray* v *DPP* [1994] 1 WLR 1, at page 12, Lord Slynn of Hadley declared that the trial judge (sitting, of course, without a jury) '. . . was . . . entitled to have regard to the circumstantial evidence as a whole and *to conclude that a refusal to deal with it, or any of it, justified an inference of guilt*' (emphasis added).

So there it is — from the mouth of one of the country's most distinguished lawyers: a refusal by an accused person to answer the evidence brought against him or her can justify an inference of guilt.

It is, of course, a constitutional change of the most major significance, pushed through Parliament in the teeth of opposition and protest from the Bar Council, the Law Society, the Criminal Bar Association, JUSTICE, Liberty, Senior Treasury Counsel at the Old Bailey — and even the Chairman of the Royal Commission on Criminal Justice. But this is how things are done in today's Britain. We don't have a written Constitution, our much-trumpeted checks and balances have decayed to the point where they no longer work, and a whipped, misguided, parliamentary majority is free to make hay with British liberties whenever it suits their political purposes. This is what has happened.

And we lawyers — every self-respecting, sentient, British lawyer who knows anything about the history of this nation and who actually knows how our forefathers won the British freedoms and protections we take for granted — every lawyer who can see the danger, whether judge, prosecutor or defender — *we* have to salvage whatever we can from this parliamentary affront to our system and to our Liberty. The insolence of the politicians, pushing through this constitutional change in the face of the united opposition of every significant legal body or association in the land, is *just* the kind of abuse of power our forefathers sought to control. If the Executive can ride roughshod over the urgent warnings of the combined legal professions, the Crown's senior prosecutor *and* the chairman of the Royal Commission that investigated the whole question — what kind of responsible government does this suggest? What kind of restraints do the British people have left, with which to control the Executive? This is the kind of thing Cromwell went to war with Charles I about.

It is now up to the judges and to prosecuting and defending advocates to save what *can* be saved of this abandoned British liberty. And it would be a proud day for us common lawyers if we succeeded in preserving it and restoring it to the British people. For we *could* do it, and do it quite triumphantly. It is all within our discretion whether we stoop to use these new powers of comment. Many judges are going to view with distaste the idea of warning an accused person in a British court that if he doesn't actively try to defend himself, this will count towards proving his guilt. For that is what the judges may well have to do — warn the accused in open court — 'speak, or run a greater risk of conviction' — and many of them won't like it.

As for the prosecutors of England and Wales, they are, by and large, an immensely honourable group of people. Most of them would hate the idea of being the first lawyer in England or in the Principality to comment on the silence of the accused. If the prosecutors *and* the judges, out of respect for and understanding of this threatened liberty, simply decline to comment on the silence of the accused, all may yet be well.

Are we up to the task? If we are not, and if the accused's failure to give an account of himself becomes commented on as a matter of practice, then we are headed into a minefield of difficulties. Take the simplest scenario. The accused says the prosecution witnesses are lying: sometimes this is not just the only defence available, sometimes it happens to be the truth. If the accused is of previous bad character, and if he gives evidence himself, in goes his character. It is all but unavoidable. Under this new law he is effectively forced into the witness box where he is almost bound to be cross-examined as to his previous convictions.

Making it all but inevitable that evidence of previous convictions will be *the norm* is a fundamental change in our criminal process: by pre-1994 standards it is an affront to our concept of a fair trial. How we handle this problem, if comments start to be made about the accused's failure to speak in his own defence, is going to be problematic. And because this is just *one* example of the difficulties we are heading for, the appeal courts are going to be even busier than they already are. We will have to see how things develop, and keep our fingers crossed that the collective wisdom of bench and bar will save the day.

PACE, in 1984, was a happy exception to our general drift away from our earlier, higher, standards. As a result of this excellent Act, the resistance to tape-recorded and/or videotaped interrogations was overcome, and our system of criminal justice is no longer besmirched by completely uncorroborated oral 'confessions'. But PACE was the exception that probed the rule. At the time of writing it looks as if further diminishments of our rights are on the stocks — the accused's right to elect trial by jury in 'either-way' offences seems about to disappear — at the unanimous recommendation of the Royal Commission.

We are living through a dangerous time in our nation's history. The civil law is already inaccessible to more than half the population — they either can't afford it or they can't get legal aid — we are throwing away our criminal protections with both hands and we have lost virtually all control over high-handed Executive action. We are still smarting from the shameful miscarriages of justice that came to light in recent years — the Guildford Four, the Birmingham Six, Judith Ward etc — and respect for the law in Britain is nothing like what it was, and ought to be. Lord Nolan, one of our Lords of Appeal in Ordinary, put it simply and succinctly in a recent interview. 'I have always thought,' he said, 'that unless the man in the street has a sufficient respect for the law, then one can forget all about it'. By 'it' he seemed to mean the sum of things, the British way of life.

As we approach the millennium, therefore, we lawyers, and particularly we advocates, have a heavy responsibility. If we fail to recognise that British justice is under severe threat, and if *we* don't try to do something about it, there's no-one else who will. It bears repeating: we are in desperate need of excellent, fearless, advocates.

In producing the new edition of this book I have been enormously assisted by the advice and practical guidance of my son, Charles Evans. His six years in practice at the London Bar have enabled him to up-date me on what it is like for today's young advocate, and on the many changes that have come about since this Beginner's Guide was first written. I must emphasise, however, that I take full responsibility for the views expressed in this book. I also want to acknowledge, with warmth and gratitude, the constant support of Alistair MacQueen and Heather Saward of Blackstone Press — in my experience, probably the most vigorous and imaginative law publishers in the English-speaking world today.

Keith Evans
Gray's Inn, January 1995

Preface to the First Edition

We were hurtling along a bit of road between Kingston and Gray's Inn. I think it was somewhere in Wandsworth but it felt like one of the straighter bits of the bypass. I was musing contentedly that history was repeating itself. Here I was, a helpless passenger, being dramatically transported from court to chambers in a small fast car driven by my pupil. I remembered how, as a pupil, I had done the same thing with my master, how he too had sat twitching as I was doing now, while we rocketed back to the Temple.

Fair enough, I was thinking to myself. Sitting there in court all day, listening, writing furiously but getting the chance to say nothing at all, a pupil understandably needs to let off steam, and if snap gear changes and a spot of 3G acceleration is what he feels like . . .. Well, if the Good Lord wills it we'll get back to chambers in one piece. He spoke.

'Something's been puzzling me', he said.
'Oh. What's that?'
'I can't work out why you winced when N—— asked the judge to send the jury out.'
'*I winced?*'
'Oh yes.'
'What, *visibly?*'
'Yes.'
'Oh dear', I said. 'That's bad.'
'Why so?'
'Because I didn't know I'd done it and if I risked conveying something by my facial expression that I didn't intend to convey I wasn't doing my job properly. Do you think the jury noticed?'
'I don't think so. They were looking at an exhibit. Is it that important?'
'Of course it is. Haven't I ever talked to you about this?'

'No.'

'I haven't said anything about facial expression in court?'

'No.'

'And how much pupillage have you done with me?'

'Eight months.'

'And I obviously haven't told you about getting the jury out of court either?'

'No, you haven't.'

I sat there, thinking, as we smartly changed lanes and overtook a Jaguar on the inside.

'Have I talked to you about . . . ?'

'No.'

'Or about . . . ?'

'No.'

'Then what *have* I been teaching you?

He was very solicitous and comforting. He started to pick off the dozens of things that we *had* discussed, that I *had* thought of telling him. But what became so desperately clear was that far more had been left out than had been included.

It was out of this quite accidental conversation that I became aware of the need for me to make a checklist of the things that I really ought to explain to my pupils if I was to be in any way fair to them. I began to jot things down as they occurred to me and as I did I began to feel more and more guilty, more and more angry with myself and with the system. I felt as if I had hardly taught them a thing, my pupils. There had been virtually no planning, nothing systematic. I had let them go along picking up what they could and I had given no thought as to whether we had covered *anything* let alone everything.

And the checklist got bigger. Lines grew into paragraphs as explanations were called for, and the pages began to multiply. It wasn't a question of asking myself: 'what next?' There was so much totally basic material that I should have been passing on to my pupils, so much that was perfectly obvious to me and my contemporaries at the Bar. But it couldn't possibly be obvious to a beginner. So I kept on jotting and scribbling, trying to get down just the essentials. And in this way the book more or less wrote itself.

But one feels very, very diffident about 'going public'. One is understandably nervous that one's contemporaries will say something like: 'who does he think he is, setting himself up as some kind of authority on advocacy?' So let me insist that I am doing nothing of the kind. This is just one advocate's attempt to systematise what he feels he ought to have been trying to pass on to his pupils over the years. People who looked at bits of what I had written were kind enough to say that it ought to be finished and ought to be offered for publication. My old friend, Peter Murphy, whose book on Evidence is proving so useful to English law students everywhere, *told* me to show the manuscript to his publishers. Their enthusiasm was very encouraging, and with astonishing speed what started so recently as my checklist is now a book.

I *do* offer it with diffidence and I hope it will be of some real use to the beginner.

I want to say thank you to a number of people: to Alistair, John, Heather and Pat who, from the publishers' side of things, took a manuscript and turned it into a book; to my wife, Anna, the writer in my family, whose cryptic advice on editing was invaluable; to my ex-pupil, John, who in one long afternoon in San Francisco, added so many ideas to the manuscript; to Chris who started the whole thing and who still drives in the same manner; to Nigel, to whom I always turned when I needed confirmation; to . . .. Not having ever tried this exercise before I hadn't realised how many people I want to thank. I had better stop — noting with emphasis that *inclusio unius* does not mean *exclusio alterius* — and let you get on with the book.

Keith Evans
Gray's Inn, February 1983

PART ONE

THE BASIC TOOLS
OF ADVOCACY

One

Introduction

In recent years the legal professions of the English-speaking world have been expanding rapidly. In the 1980s and early 1990s young barristers in England and Wales were qualifying at the rate of something like 1,000 a year. On current figures, there will be, each year, at least 800 new barristers on the market. Some of these will return to the Commonwealth countries from which they came, but the majority will stay in England and Wales. They will either look for jobs in commerce or industry or they will take the next step to becoming practising barristers: they will try to find pupillage.

If they find it, they will spend an aggregate of at least twelve months in somebody's chambers, watching how law is actually practised. Depending on their luck, the teaching they receive during pupillage will be good, mediocre or virtually non-existent. Again, depending on their luck, they might or might not, during their second six months, get into court and hear the sound of their own voices. The lucky pupil will find himself or herself in company with a pupil master who enjoys teaching and whose example is a good one, and in chambers where, at the end of their 'first six', pupils regularly get sent to the magistrates' courts to adjourn cases, to make simple bail applications, to deal with pleas of guilty and perhaps even to handle simple fights. If the pupillage chambers have a mixed practice, he or she may be sent before the Master in Chambers, doing simple applications, and before county court judges on any number of small matters.

The odd thing is, however, that the pupil will have received a very curious training for all this. He or she will be standing there in court, looking to the world like a real-life barrister. Yet the pupil master sees virtually none of this, will never have heard the pupil speak in court, will never have had the opportunity of saying, 'No, no, That's *not* the way to do it!', will never have the chance of correcting the pupil's glaring errors and blundering early steps.

And why not? Because the system makes no provision for it. The pupil master is busy and when he is in court his client expects *him* to ask the questions, to address the judge and do the talking. Rarely, very rarely does the chance arise when one can safely say to one's pupil: 'I want you to take the next witness: just ask him so and so'. I was able to do this just three times in eighteen years. And even if the master does get the chance of standing the pupil on his feet to break his duck with a few terrified sentences, the chance that he will be able to watch him do it again is almost non-existent. What happens in busy chambers is that the 'second six' pupil will be sent off to court to learn by trial and error, and if the public realised just how little we have done as a profession to train our newcomers, there would be a justifiable outcry.

It is shameful to think how little proper training has been available for the pupil. Can it be imagined that a new dentist could begin to practise without ever having extracted a tooth or done a filling but only watched them being done? Or that a new anaesthetist might be permitted to put a patient under when his only experience was book-learning and observation? Or that a student pilot might be allowed even one circuit of the airfield solo without many hours of trying to do it under the watchful eye of an instructor? It would be dangerous to let such a pilot or such a dentist or such an anaesthetist loose on an unsuspecting public. People might get killed. So it might be said, a pupil's incompetence won't kill anybody. True, but it might lead the client to gaol, it might lead to the loss of a driving licence that in turn leads to unemployment and perhaps bankruptcy, and it not only might, but does lead to cases being lost that should have been won and to the innocent being convicted.

The beginner-advocate has been, for centuries, a licensed amateur, knowing very little of the skills needed to do the job properly.

England is not alone in this. America is even worse. There the new arrival can set up on the day he qualifies without any pupillage at all. And indeed it is generally accepted throughout the English-speaking world that the standards of the English Bar are by and large among the best. But as many a juryman and magistrate will tell you, that isn't saying much. Great advocacy is still very much to be found at the English Bar but our general standards, especially among the younger members have never been high enough. In the 1990s we are about to see great changes in the formal teaching of trial advocacy. We *could* be about to see a great raising of standards all round.

In the meantime this book ought to help get you started. It is an attempt to set out the more obvious things that need to be known about advocacy. If you go along unaided you will, within a couple of years, have worked out a lot of conscious or unconscious rules for yourself. You will have done this by making mistakes and remembering not to make them next time. You will have picked up ideas from listening to other people and you will have done a lot of thinking as you lick your wounds on the way back to chambers or office.

But you are bound to be assisted if you have some sort of map, some kind of manual, some sort of rule-book to get you started. This, if you like, is such a rule-book. It will not teach you to be a great advocate. What it certainly will do is help you not to be an embarrassment to yourself and to the profession that you have chosen to enter.

And be clear about this: in writing this book I do not set myself up as any kind of authority or lay any claim to having anything other than average powers of advocacy myself. There are several hundred practising barristers who might have written this book. We all share in having started by making the usual ghastly mistakes, in not knowing what words to use, what to do in this situation or that, when to shut up and when to persist. We have all bored the jury and appalled the client and let ourselves down badly just as you will. So try, with the help of this short handbook, to do a bit better than we did when starting. It ought not to be difficult.

At all times realise that you are your client's advocate. Think about advocacy, talk about advocacy, read about advocacy. If you don't find it fascinating, what are you doing, starting in this profession? Learn the rules as best you can and when you have learnt them be ready to break them. Look for new and better ways of doing the job. Regard it as a craft that has to be learnt but never lose sight of the fact that it is an art as well. Learn your trade. Aim to become a craftsman. Aspire to become an artist.

There are very few modern books on advocacy. There are some turn of the century works from America which make good background reading and in the United States today there are publications produced by Continuing Education of the Bar schemes which deal with different aspects of trial conduct. A modern book which you *must* read is the late Richard Du Cann's *Art of the Advocate* (Penguin, 3rd edition, 1982). It is a very different kind of book from this one. He and I approach the subject from very different directions. This book aims to tell you about the nuts and bolts of the trade while his book illustrates the true art that advocacy can rise to. Read it and enjoy it. Remember the names of the great advocates mentioned in it. Get to know who Marshall Hall, Rufus Isaacs, Norman Birkett and Pat Hastings were. Another book which I can highly recommend is *Advocacy Skills* by Judge Michael Hyam (Blackstone Press, 2nd edition, 1992). Again, it takes a very different approach: pay particular attention to Hyam's chapter on pleas in mitigation.

Too many law students these days don't seem to know much history. They are missing out on a lot of sheer pleasure because of that. (Why is a solicitor so called?) Familiarise yourselves with the 'greats' of the past. There are excellent biographies and memoirs of those advocates, and although styles change you can learn a lot from their careers. There really ought to be no single Bar student looking for a pupillage who cannot say at once who it was that asked: 'What is the coefficient of expansion of brass?', or who it was that began a lethal cross-examination with the stark little question: 'Did you like her?' It is, of course, possible to become a good advocate without much knowledge of the past but an awareness of it can do nothing but good.

So much, then, by way of introduction. Let us get down to practicalities. 'Technique' is a Greek word that means a bag of tools. We shall start to look at some of those tools.

Two

Court etiquette

This chapter consists of a mixed bag of hints and explanations on the subject of being in court and of addressing tribunals. The newcomer often gets confused by the unfamiliar language and finds himself tongue-tied because he cannot find the appropriate phrase. He often comes to grief in other, trivial ways, which can be so easily avoided. Learn early on that what may seem trivial might be of importance. Do not scorn to take note of little conventions and, at first, to follow them. Courtesy, if you think about it, means the kind of manners that are used at court. Whether that means the court at which the monarch gives audience or the law court where the monarch's representatives hear and determine cases does not really matter. The manners ought to be the same. Those manners have lasted as long as they have because they perform an enormously important function: they turn what would otherwise be a brawl of an argument into a civilised means of getting as near to the truth as the rules of evidence permit. So let us look at the manners of the law court.

Begin with this thought: the law court wields authority and power. Whether that court consists of just one person, like the Queen's Bench judge or stipendiary magistrate, or of several, like the five Lords of Appeal in Ordinary or the three Lords Justices in the Court of Appeal, that one judge or group of judges, or lay justices in the magistrates' courts, represent the ultimate authority in that court. And this kind of authority demands the outward appearance of respect from those who come before it. Whether the court actually does command your respect or not is strictly irrelevant. Always attempt to behave towards the court as if you do feel respect for it. This does not mean that you have to cringe or toady. It does mean that part of your mind must always be concerned to maintain that appearance of respect. In time, like so many other things, this will become subconscious, a habit. But as you start out be sure to bear this in mind. How should it be done?

Dress and personal appearance

Remember that fashions change slowly in the courts. While blue jeans may now be acceptable dress in many walks of life the advocate is expected to wear a certain kind of uniform. Until a man is of several years' call he should turn up to no court in anything other than a dark, three-piece suit. You can get away with a two-piece suit if it is double-breasted and if you keep it buttoned. At all costs cover your front stud. Have a handkerchief in your breast pocket, not pens. Do not wear a loud tie. Make sure that you are brushed down and that your shoes are clean. You can wear your hair as you want to, within reason, but again, make sure that it is clean and tidy.

All this is *far* more important than you may care to admit at the outset. Follow these rules slavishly until you have been around the courts long enough to judge for yourself. Speaking to the woman reader for a moment let me quote from the first edition of this book, in 1983. This is how things stood: 'There are now far more women in practice than there have ever been. It is probably true to say that, except for the older clerks and solicitors, you are now accepted on an entirely or almost entirely equal footing with men; and things are improving all the time. The battle that the feminist movement has had to wage, and is still waging, has won a lot of quiet victories in the legal professions.'

This is now history, and I think it is fair to say that the battle has been well and truly won. Although there is no equality of numbers, the old prejudices against women in the legal professions seem to have disappeared almost entirely. The advice given here merely describes the standards of successful women lawyers. (Incidentally, if in the rest of this book the masculine is often used to include the feminine it is done to avoid clumsy expression and for no other reason.) In court you should wear dark clothes, keep the jewellery to a minimum and your hair looking like a TV advertisement. Aim to appear businesslike and well groomed but don't be afraid to be feminine and attractive at the same time.

Both men and women barristers, when robed for court, should make sure that the wig covers all the hair at the forehead and that the linen around the throat is clean and uncrumpled. Never wear dark brown or green in court; the right colours are black, dark blue or grey. The only exception in this: it is an agreeable affectation of the more senior barrister sometimes to turn up at the magistrate's court wearing a slightly countrified outfit. Rather like using a lectern in court, you will know when you are senior enough to do it. Do please remember that the whole business of your appearance does matter. You face enough difficulties at the outset without alienating your court by scruffy characteristics or flashy dressing.

What should the solicitor-advocate wear when appearing in the higher courts or county courts? There has been a Practice Direction on this — [1994] 1 WLR 1056 — which says that solicitors shall wear a black stuff gown with bands but no wig. Although the Practice Direction doesn't say as much, it is implicit that the gown should be worn over suitably dark clothing.

Posture in court

Nonchalance is a great thing and the time may come when you will use it to advantage. To start with, avoid it like the plague. Try not to let too much show on your face. Judges say that facial expressions convey a great deal and your task is to give away nothing unless you intend to. Particularly bear this in mind when you are in pupillage. Gleeful expressions on your part as your master scores a point or horrified ones as he loses will do nothing but harm to his case. It is not

suggested that you sit there like a stuffed dummy but bear in mind what can be revealed by the human face and its changes. We will come back to this later in the book.

When you address the court stand up and stand straight. Never put your hand in your pocket except perhaps a thumb in your waistcoat pocket. By all means play with your pen as you address the court but make sure that you do not distract your audience by doing this — and *never* click the pen! When in robes you will find that, without trying, you will be adopting those physical twitches that actors try to imitate when playing barristers. Your gown will slide off your shoulder and you will tweak it back, catching the pigtails of your wig and you will then tweak them. Just try to keep this to an absolute minimum while talking to the court or to the jury. And remember, when anyone is taking the oath, you freeze. Do not move and certainly do not speak until the oathtaking is finished.

Modes of address

In the days when every lawyer had done at least a little Latin everybody understood the difference between the nominative case and the vocative. Brutus became Brute as Caesar's last word on the subject. The vocative lives on in the way we address some judges. But let us look first at who gets called what.

'My Lord' or 'My Lady' is the proper title for the following:

(a)   Lords of Appeal in Ordinary — the House of Lords;
(b)   Lords Justices — the Court of Appeal;
(c)   High Court judges and any deputy sitting as a High Court judge;
(d)   all persons sitting as judges at the Central Criminal Court — Old Bailey;

There is a mystery as to whether 'My Lord' or 'Your Honour' is appropriate for:

(e)   the judge of the Liverpool Court of Passage;
(f)   any Circuit Judge who holds the honorary office of Recorder of Liverpool or Recorder of Manchester. Check locally!

'Your Honour', which suffices both for men and women, is the proper title for the following:

(a) all circuit judges whether sitting in the Crown Court or in the County Court, together with their deputies, unless they appear in the list above;
(b) recorders and deputy recorders;
(c) most other judges throughout the Commonwealth and the United States.

Everybody else is called 'Master', 'Sir', or 'Madam/Ma'am'. Let us deal with each of these in turn.

'My Lord' Those two words are usually used in the vocative case. You are effectively calling your judge by his official name. 'So you see, Sir, that is the position', becomes 'So you see, My Lord, that is the position'. The title causes a little confusion, however, because of its alternative uses. Let me illustrate:

'My Lord, I don't know if Your Lordship has had the opportunity of seeing the papers in this matter?'

Work on the basis, at the outset, that you never refer to a judge as plain 'you'. Always call him 'Your Lordship' when you would otherwise want to say 'you'. Likewise, never refer to the judge as 'him' or 'her'. You should say to the witness, 'Tell his Lordship what happened after that', or 'Tell her Ladyship about the incidents of the following evening'. You could also say, 'Tell the learned judge what happened next', but it is slightly better to use 'his Lordship' and 'her Ladyship'.

What you *must* avoid is confusing the use of 'Your Lordship' with the vocative when speaking directly to him. It is wrong to begin by saying, 'Your Lordship, I do not know' etc. Instead you should say, 'My Lord, I do not know' etc. This may seem elementary, and it is, but mistakes of this kind are terribly common.

There is still another way in which the words 'My Lord' can be used. As an alternative to 'Tell his Lordship' etc, you can say 'Tell My Lord' etc. This is not at all uncommon, and those of you who know Latin will see that it is the dative or arguably accusative use of the words.

Summarising these often confusing little linguistic rules, we therefore
have the following equivalents:

Sir	My Lord
Madam	My Lady
him	his Lordship, or My Lord
her	her Ladyship, or My Lady
you	Your Lordship, or Your Ladyship

There are other correct variations but if you understand what has been
set out here you will be able to work them out for yourself. Let us have
a short illustration to tie these ideas together.

> 'My Lord, I propose asking the witness to write down the answer to
> my next question. I don't know if that would commend itself to Your
> Lordship?'
> 'Certainly, Mr Snooks.'
> 'So be it, My Lord. You heard what his Lordship said, Mr Smith.
> Will you please write down the answer to my question and have the
> usher hand it to My Lord?'
> 'Before you ask the question, Mr Snooks, do I have a copy of this
> witness's second statement?'
> 'My Lord, I think not, but I have a spare copy for Your Lordship.
> Usher, will you be kind enough to hand this to the learned judge.'

I hope this makes it clear. Do try to get it right. Mistakes in such
fundamental matters tend to stick out like a sore thumb.

'*Your Honour*' is easier. It serves for both 'my Lord' and 'Your
Lordship' and, indeed, for 'My Lady' and 'Your Ladyship'. For
example:

> 'Your Honour, I don't know if Your Honour has had the opportunity
> of seeing the deposition, since I believe it was omitted from Your
> Honour's bundle?'
> 'No, Mr Snooks.'
> 'Then I shall have a copy made and, if I may, take Your Honour to
> the relevant parts of it when that has been done.'

When referring to this judge as 'him' you use the words 'his Honour'.
The 'her' equivalent is, obviously, 'her Honour'.

All that remains to be said about 'Your Honour' and 'My Lord' is that you ought to make absolutely sure that you are employing the right title. No judge is so petty as to make a big thing out of it, but, again, it sticks out like the proverbial sore thumb if you address a judge who ought to be 'My Lord' as 'Your Honour' and vice versa.

'Master' is a title accorded to the Queen's Bench Master and the Chancery Master and you use the word where you would normally use 'Sir'. We do not have a woman occupying that office yet and no doubt there will be a Practice Direction on how to address her if the need arises. With the Master have no reluctance to call him 'you'. If you have occasion to need the equivalent of 'him' you would use the words 'the Master', but somehow it never seems necessary. If you use the word 'Master' as an intelligent sixth former would use the word 'Sir' when talking to his headmaster you won't go far wrong.

Sir and Madam Barristers never call magistrates 'Your Worship'; solicitors often do. It is one of those odd little distinctions between the two sides of the profession, but it is not uncommon to hear solicitors these days dropping 'Your Worship' from their vocabulary. Indeed, it is to be anticipated that barristers and solicitors, from now on, will adopt the same modes of address for the bench. If you are addressing a bench of more than one magistrate then you direct your remarks to the one in the middle. Call him 'Sir'; if it is a lady chairperson call her 'Madam' or 'Ma'am'. As to this latter, the choice is yours and the practising Bar are divided on it. Some take the view that the use of 'Madam' makes the barrister sound like a sales assistant at Harrods. Another argument for 'Ma'am' (pronounced, incidentally with a short vowel — 'Mam' or 'Mem' depending on your accent) is that if it's good enough for the Queen then it's good enough for the lady chairman of the bench and she might very well prefer it. Registrars of all kinds are, by the way, called 'Sir' or 'Madam/Ma'am'.

As to all these courteous forms of address it ought to be noted that the beginner tends to overdo the use of them, punctuating his halting sentences with My Lords and Your Lordships in substitution for ums and ers. Don't do it. Use the titles often enough to indicate that you know they are the proper form of address and in order to indicate your respect for the court, but go easy on them.

Again, it is now old fashioned to the point of being comic to refer to a judge as 'M'Lud'. The 'My' is still suppressed into a vestigial 'M' sound but the 'Lord' is pronounced normally. When using 'Your Lordship', you again suppress the 'Your' into a gentle 'Yuh' sound.

How do you include the others if you are addressing a multi-person court? If you are before a bench of magistrates you talk to the chairman and refer to the existence of the others, if necessary, by calling them 'your colleagues'. This is not to infer that when addressing them you stare fixedly at the one in the middle to the exclusion of the others. You look at and talk to them all, but the one with whom you have any discussion and upon whom you should focus your remarks is the chairman. If you are before the Court of Appeal and the judge on the right has interrupted with a point that you want to refer to later then you say something like: 'I would respectfully adopt the way in which My Lord, Lord Justice Soap, expressed it a moment ago.' Or if the President of the Court — the one in the middle — has raised something that you want to refer back to, you say something like: 'If I could return to the point raised by My Lord, Lord Justice Bloggs . . .'. The same goes for the House of Lords, but don't worry about that for the immediate future.

The use of the word 'learned'

Understand that it is part of the courteous language of the court and that it simply means 'qualified as a lawyer'. When, as a barrister, you introduce your opponent to the court you call him 'my learned friend':

'I appear to prosecute in this case, Members of the Jury, while the defendant is represented by my learned friend, Mr Snooks.'

After that and for the rest of the case you can, and a lot of practitioners do, refer to your opponent just as 'm'friend'. If you are ever addressing a judge or a magistrate, any tribunal indeed, and you have occasion to refer to a judge who is elsewhere, you always refer to him as 'the learned judge' or 'the learned Lord Justice'. Likewise, when in the Court of Appeal you are seeking to overturn the ruling of the judge in the court below, he is always referred to as 'the learned trial judge' or 'the learned judge' or 'the learned recorder'. Funnily enough, you do not use the expression 'the learned trial recorder'. Should you find yourself in the House of Lords and trying to upset a decision of the

Lord Chief Justice himself — which can happen — he is referred to by you as 'the learned Lord Chief Justice'. In similar fashion, the clerk in the magistrates' court is often qualified and is in any event assumed to be: he or she is therefore referred to when you are addressing the bench as 'your learned clerk'. Do not make the mistake, however, of referring to the other magistrates on the lay bench as 'your learned colleagues'. Justices of the peace may very well be qualified in all manner of things but it is unlikely that they are qualified in the law and they are assumed not to be. Thus they do not qualify for the description 'learned'. *A fortiori,* do not perpetuate the endearing mistake, some-times heard, of referring to 'the learned usher'. I did know an usher once who had a degree in physics from Oxford along with a 2:1 in law from London and who subsequently got qualified at the English, Texas and California Bars. It would still, in the circumstances, have been fundamental error to have called her 'the learned usher'.

For no particularly evident reason, the one person who, although being qualified in law, used not to be referred to as 'learned' was the solicitor. A barrister opposed by a solicitor did not refer to him as a learned friend, or friend even. He was alluded to as Mr whatever his name was. Now that solicitors have extended rights of audience it may well turn out that *all* advocates will refer to each other as 'my friend', but only time will tell. Be on the lookout for what develops and act accordingly.

As to language generally

We are still dealing here with the 'manners' that your being in court requires of you. With regard to the kind of language you ought to use it is possible to indicate a few basic ground rules. They can all be broken but they provide a useful starting point.

Try to avoid asking the judge a direct question. If you want to know if he is ready to break for lunch the way to ask is by saying, 'I wonder if that would be a convenient moment, Your Honour'. If you want an adjournment you can wonder again:

'I wonder if Your Lordship would be kind enough to rise for perhaps ten minutes. A matter has arisen on which I really must take instructions.'

'Well, can't you deal with that at the adjournment, Mr Snooks? We really must get on.'

'My Lord, I really do hesitate to trouble Your Lordship in this way but it seems to me a matter of some importance.'

'Oh very well, Mr Snooks, but be as quick as you can. Let me know when you are ready.'

'I really am most grateful to Your Lordship.'

Another illustration:

'I don't know if Your Lordship has had the opportunity of reading the papers in this case?'

'Yes, I have, Mr Snooks.'

'I'm grateful, My Lord. In that case, Your Lordship will see that . . .'.

Do remember how useful 'I wonder . . .' and 'I don't know if . . .' can be.

Always ask the judge for his permission   You don't just stand up and start addressing him. Nor do you just get up and begin calling witnesses or addressing the jury. The judge, remember, is the ultimate authority in that court and it is a matter of courtesy to get his assent to whatever you are about to do. It is incredibly easy and it oils the wheels, adding at the same time to the impression that you know what you are about, professionally. The first thing you ever say to a judge, magistrate, master, chairman of a tribunal or president of a court martial is 'May it please you, My Lord/Your Honour/Master/Sir', or as a variation of the first of those, 'May it please Your Lordship/Your Ladyship'. Literally the words 'May it please' are the same kind of subjunctive as 'God save the Queen'. They merely express the hope that what you are about to do or say will meet with the court's approval. A close alternative to 'May it please . . .' is 'If it please. . .'. Use either phrase as an automatic starter whenever you initiate a new development in court, as for instance when you begin to address the judge in opening or in closing, when you are about to address the jury, and, perhaps now and again, when you begin a cross-examination. Certainly, if you are half way through a cross-examination when you break for the midday adjournment, you start the afternoon's proceedings with the words before resuming your questioning. When you are about to call your first witness before judge and jury and you have been addressing the jury in an opening speech, you wind up with the words, 'And now, with his Lordship's leave, I shall call the evidence before you. Mr Fagin, please.' If you have finished your opening submissions to a judge sitting without a jury you say, 'And now, if it please your Honour, I propose to call the first witness.'

Make a habit of thanking the judge for just about everything. 'Much obliged, My Lord' covers most situations. 'My Lord, I'm obliged', is perhaps a shade more elegant. 'Most grateful to Your Lordship' is a good alternative. Use them all. Stick to these phrases until you have gained a little experience. Then you will know when to use the simple, 'My Lord, thank you'. If he interrupts you wait until he has finished talking and then, before you answer him, throw in an 'I'm obliged, My Lord' as a preliminary. If he criticises you even, you often do well to start again with a quiet 'My Lord, I'm obliged'. In situations where it would obviously be silly to use the phrases, as for instance where the judge says, 'Well, I think we'll break off there, Mr Snooks', the answer is 'Very good, My Lord', or 'So be it, My Lord'.

When asking the judge to do something, ask indirectly. You want to draw his attention to a particular page. You can say, 'I wonder if Your Lordship sees page 123 of the bundle?' Carefully phrased, you *can* use a direct question, as for instance: 'Would Your Lordship be kind enough to look at page 123?' or 'Does Your Lordship see the bottom of page 123?' You can also say 'Might I refer Your Honour to page 123?' These are so much better than phrases heard at moots: 'I refer Your Lordship to. . .', or 'I would refer Your Lordship to. . .'. The recommended methods of phrasing, you notice, are much more *invitations* than directions, thus reflecting your recognition that the judge is, in court, the ultimate authority and not to be *told* what anyone is going to do. Thus phrases such as 'I would invite . . .' and 'Perhaps Your Lordship would be good enough to . . .' are particularly useful. If all this sounds terribly unctuous, don't worry. It is nothing of the sort. It is the kind of politeness which has been used for centuries. There is no humbling oneself involved. Your judge did exactly the same when he was at the Bar and in a rapidly changing world it is one of the old-fashioned things that still has a totally up-to-date function.

Stick to dictionary language. Treat slang and even commonly accepted abbreviations with infinite care. Well within living memory there

was a judge at the Old Bailey who abhorred the word 'taxi': he insisted
that in his court that well known means of getting about be referred to
as a 'taximetered cabriolet'! Times have changed a bit since then but
there are still judges who won't tolerate the word 'pub': it has to be
'public house'. Let somebody else be the first to use the word, see how
the judge reacts and adjust accordingly. It is generally safe, however,
to adopt the use of a shortened word or phrase if it has first been used
by a witness. Thus, if the witness had been talking about what
happened 'down the pub', it would be pompous of the advocate to start
referring to 'the public house': he can safely use the slang version.

Take care with your language and realise that if you practise these
archaic methods of speech you will pick them up quite quickly. You
may even come to like them. Certainly if you get the right idiom as
quickly as possible you are well on the way to concealing from your
court and client that you may still be a bit wet behind the ears.

To wind up this chapter, be aware of a strange little courtesy and of an
odd little rule of conduct. The courtesy is this. If a judge is sitting in
court in robes, then the Bar thinks he ought not to be abandoned. If
you are the last barrister sitting there, you don't get up and go until he
has told you to. This polite staying around, doing nothing, is called
'dressing the court'. Judges know the rule and will excuse you with the
words: 'Please don't wait, Mr Snooks'. At this you stand, say 'Your
Lordship's most kind', or 'If it please you, My Lord', bow and leave
the court. If there are two of you, you both wait. If within fifteen
seconds the judge hasn't given you the let out you can get up and say,
'I wonder if Your Lordship would be kind enough to excuse me: I
ought to be elsewhere'. He almost certainly will.

The little rule of conduct is that a barrister in robes never carries a
brief-case or any other kind of bag. Where the rule comes from I don't
know: it is probably that until recent times barristers usually had clerks
in fairly constant attendance if they were successful. Anyway, carrying
a bag or a case of any kind just isn't done and looks odd to the rest of
the Bar. If you see people in wig and gown carrying brief-cases, they
are probably salaried officials of the court and not practising barristers.
The rule does not apply when you are not wearing robes, but habits die
hard and barristers are rarely seen to take brief-cases into court. They
tend to leave them in counsel's room. In New South Wales the rule is

stricter. Silks there are not even allowed to carry papers. Again, therefore, check locally to find out whether you are complying with the club rules.

Very well. That should be enough, by way of preliminaries, to keep you out of immediate trouble. Let us attempt now to formulate some general rules about basic advocacy.

Three

The jury

It is difficult to satisfactorily systematise a book about advocacy. This makes it radically different from just about any other law book you have read or browsed through. You have got used to seeing law books laid out in defined headings and chapters and have grown accustomed to thinking of law as the kind of discipline that can be neatly compartmentalised, indexed and ordered. Advocacy is a subject that does not allow of such convenient filleting. As we proceed in this book there will be a number of 'rules' proposed. Some will strike you as obvious, some less so. There is nothing sacred about any of them, and they have not been garnered out of some classic work on advocacy or rhetoric.

The rules which appear in this book are guidelines that have been picked up by watching other advocates at work over the last thirty years and by trying to do it myself. None of us puts all the rules into operation: the art or craft of advocacy is too individual a business to allow of that. But it seems useful that you should have some rules formulated for you and explained. This way you will know what to be on the look-out for when you first go to court as a spectator, and you will have some idea of what you ought to be aiming for when you first get into court in your own right. In among the exposition of the rules you will find a great deal of other material that cannot be helpfully indexed, information as to what you *may* do and information as to what you *must* do. Remember that this is not a short book on civil or criminal procedure, nor is it a book on evidence. These you must know well if you are going to be a useful advocate, particularly evidence, and it is assumed that you know where to look for your law in these subjects.

Until comparatively recently most English-speaking advocacy, both civil and criminal, was conducted in front of a jury. This is still the case in America, but in Britain the powers that be have so arranged things that the civil jury has all but vanished. If a British advocate, therefore, wants to follow our centuries-old tradition of appearing in front of juries, the only way one can do it is by including criminal work in one's practice. When this book first appeared, one reviewer regretted that so much of it was written from the standpoint of the criminal trial. But since the criminal jury is, to all intents and purposes, the only jury left to us, we *have* to learn our jury advocacy in a criminal context. Be assured, however, that the differences between civil jury advocacy and criminal jury advocacy are negligible. Well over sixty per cent of the entire court-room time of the Bar in England, taken as a whole, is given over to Crown Court crime. The whole of the law of evidence grew up because of the great use that has been made of juries throughout the centuries, and it was in front of juries that almost all the great advocacy of the past took place. For this reason we will look at the dos and don'ts of jury advocacy first, acknowledging that you won't get the chance of actually addressing a jury yourself for some little time yet. The basic rules and hints set out here will apply to your advocacy before other tribunals as well, subject to the important modifications that we will deal with in later chapters.

Four basic guidelines

This is not the place to discuss the history of the jury. Suffice it to say that its use is very ancient indeed and that the members of the public who are picked off the voters' register to do their two or three week stint of jury service are performing one of the oldest duties of the English or Commonwealth or American citizen. Do bear in mind, however, that the vast majority of them are totally unaware of this. As far as they are concerned the whole thing is probably a chore, it is often a thundering nuisance and it is a bore for a lot of the time. Since the qualifications for jury service are so slight you get literally all types called to be jurors. They tend to be a real cross-section of society and, numerically, they represent the different strata in society as well. It is important to remember this. The advertising agencies have got society classified into groups and, with the ultimate objective of making money, they aim their product at the group they want to reach. They pigeon-hole us all into high or medium or low grades of intelligence, learning, perception, taste, gullibility, purchasing power and the rest. They not only recognise that people are not all born equal: they make a science of understanding it. And to some extent so should you. A lot of the jury men and women that you will address are going to be ill-educated and some of them not all that far from illiterate.

Never forget this. Never. I heard a barrister at the Old Bailey when I was a pupil say to a bewildered jury of East-Enders, 'You may think, Members of the Jury, that it is the peripheral indicia which will ultimately lead to the resolution of this case'. And at the very end of the 1950s senior Treasury Counsel asked another Old Bailey jury if they would let their wives and servants read *Lady Chatterley's Lover*.

Those are just two somewhat extreme illustrations of what British advocates do all the time. They imitate each other, pick up the time-worn old phrases that barristers and judges use and have been using for generations, and they direct them mindlessly at people pulled into jury service from shopfloor, nightwatchman's hut and farm.

  'The facts of this case, Members of the Jury, fall within a very small compass . . .'
  ('What's the fellow talking about a compass for? Is there a ship in the case?')
  'At the end of the day, Members of the Jury, you may very well conclude . . .'
  ('End of the day? The judge said we'd be away by dinnertime!')

For all this, juries are anything but stupid. Make no mistake about that. There is some sort of alchemy that comes about when a small crowd of twelve people gather together in odd and unfamiliar circumstances and are asked to decide something. They usually manage to do everything that justice could hope of them. The jury is a special kind of animal, a canny, shrewd and reliable animal. It is a clever beast, not to be handled carelessly. It can turn on you in a flash. Losing a jury is one of the most helplessly unpleasant sensations: watching someone else lose the jury is, equally, an unpleasant spectacle, though it must be admitted that when it is your opponent doing it your sympathy will be tinged with a measure of glee.

So when you talk to those twelve people, talk to them in language and in an idiom that they will understand, that they will feel at ease with. You can do this without the slightest sacrifice of elegance or of courtesy. The English language lends itself to simplicity and loses nothing by it. As an extreme example go and read the judgments of Lord Denning, any of them. In particular read *Jarvis* v *Swans Tours Ltd* [1973] 1 All ER 71. If you can keep your language easily understandable then not only will you get through to the less educated and less intelligent on the jury: you will also get through to the bank manager, professor of economics, or company director that you may, unknowingly, find sitting there before you.

So here we have a first and fundamental rule of advocacy: *decide whom you are talking to and adjust your language and approach to your audience.* A company chairman delivering an annual report to worried shareholders in the afternoon and making an after-dinner speech at his cricket club on the same evening would be a fool, and probably a crashing bore as well, if he adopted the same approach on both occasions. The rule may strike you as so obvious as not to need stating, but it would appal you to see how many professional advocates proceed as if it had never occurred to them.

Remember, too, that we have all been brought up to feel that being told a story is a nice experience. From early schooldays we loved it when

the teacher said, in the afternoon, 'Now we are going to have a story'. Television is catering for the same human need; and of all stories, whether on television or in the theatre or in the cinema, the court-room drama has always been regarded as being sure-fire entertainment. You have in a jury a captive audience. They would love to feel that instead of sitting there, listening to boring old evidence, they could be entertained. So entertain them. I don't mean that you should start behaving like a stand-up comic or like an actor in a melodrama.

What I do mean is that you should observe a second rule of advocacy: *strive to keep the interest of your audience.* Watch them, every one of them. If you cannot do anything positive to keep their attention and interest, you can certainly do your best to avoid losing it. Try as intently as you can not to be boring. Work at this by actively trying to identify for yourself what *you* find boring, then avoid it. What is it, in fact, that makes a person a bore? It might be the voice. Its pitch may be dreary and its tone monotonous. It might be the speed of delivery. If it is too slow the unfortunate listener may be driven wild by wanting to hurry the speaker on. On the other hand it might be too fast and perfect a delivery. I know one member of the Bar whose English is so fluent and effortless that it reels out non-stop — immaculate and at very high speed. It must look fantastic written down but to listen to it is agonising. With never a pause it goes inexorably on, fast and perfect and cultivated, until you feel that you are listening to a speeded up, accelerating record. The pressure is awful and I have seen juries wilt under its effect.

Language is not one seamless piece of cloth. It is a patchwork of words and sentences and paragraphs, and it is sewn together with pauses, changes of pace, variations in the tone of voice, and even with gesture. Look at the people who read the news on television; study their pace and their pauses. They are not practising advocacy but they are good illustrations — or some of them are — of how not to lose the interest of your audience by the wrong pace of delivery.

Another thing that tends to boredom is unsatisfactory continuity. If someone is telling a joke in a pub then no matter how good the joke may be he will lose his audience if he doesn't keep it moving. In the days when there was still variety theatre in England one of the hallmarks of a good show was the speed with which one turn followed another. As the curtain came down on one spot so there on the stage immediately appeared the link-man, filling in with a wisecrack or a song or *something* to hold the attention of the audience until the next act was ready. If you can't keep it moving for some reason or other then say something or do something to apologise for the fact. If you have mislaid your papers or can't find the note you need for your next point and you genuinely can't maintain the continuity, then tell them as much. If you must have a break in transmission, then announce it: 'Bear with me for a moment, Members of the Jury, but I really must get this right and I need to check on a note that I made.' By doing this you not only avoid boring them with your enforced pause, but you invest the pause itself with a significance of its own. It becomes part of the fabric of your endeavour before them rather than a rent in it.

And you do something else by making such a 'request'. By asking them to bear with you, you have in effect begged a favour. And everybody's best inclination, when asked 'Will you do me a favour?' is to say 'Yes, of course. What is it?' If you need something and are humble enough to ask for it, you put yourself into the position of a supplicant. You are no longer slightly inhuman in your strange dress. You turned to them and asked them for something which it was within their power to give. You have gone a little way towards demonstrating that you are as human as they are. If someone calls out 'Give us a hand!', all kindness demands that we give that hand if we can. And that strange, composite animal of the jury has an astonishing capacity for kindness if approached properly.

Which brings us to the third rule: *be as kind as you can at all times*. The tough approach is certainly called for in some situations but only very rarely. Go gently whenever you can. Try to be nice. Nothing helps more to get the truth out of a witness than a friendly and inquiring approach. Whether that witness is supposedly in your favour or against you, the person in the witness box is expecting to be 'put through it' by the advocate, especially in cross-examination. Nothing comes as a greater surprise to such a witness than to find that you are friendly, matter of fact, apologetic, when you have to suggest that he hasn't got it right; and nothing is so effective as a tool for getting what you want out of a witness.

Quite apart from the effect that the friendly approach has on the witness, think of the effect that it is bound to have on the jury. They are not, on the whole, used to thinking things through. The environment in which they live does not encourage reasoned balancing of arguments. They are far more used to 'feeling' their way through life. The advertising people know this and they aim not at the rationality of the population but at its emotions. Heineken does not refresh places that other beers cannot reach and the least intelligent in the land knows this perfectly well. But subliminally the silly and outrageous fib gets through. People are made to feel that Heineken is perhaps different in some way. The name stands out and the uncommitted drinker tries the brand. The ad-man has done his job. It's the same with sunshine breakfasts and washing powders and most other products. The appeal is to the emotions, not the mind: it is to feeling rather than to thinking.

Now the jury are being asked to think, and they will think when it is required of them. But throughout the entire proceedings they also feel, and this is something you must never forget. If they feel that you are nice and that your questions are only fair then they are likely to listen to you with much more sympathy. If you make them feel, 'Thank God, she's not cross-examining me!' then their sympathy is moving away from you and towards the witness. And a drift of sympathy, once started, is almost impossible to stop.

So here then is a fourth rule: *aim from the outset to capture and keep the sympathy of your audience.* 'Sympathy' is the Greek word, and the Latin word is 'compassion'. They both mean, literally, 'suffering along with' and they have come to mean something like having a deepish fellow feeling with another. Now think. Let us turn away from juries for a moment and put ourselves before a stipendiary magistrate. It is mid-afternoon and his list has been a heavy one. The air in the court-room is stuffy and his thoughts are getting a bit bleak. When he was at the Bar he thought of himself as an even-tempered, friendly sort and believed he'd make a decent magistrate otherwise he wouldn't have taken the job. Ten years have made him snappy and difficult. Even his wife has noticed it. He used to be able to suffer fools fairly gladly but ten years of listening to the same handful of worn-out stories over and over again have soured him. He has had not just a day or a week, but what seems a lifetime of inexperienced and unimaginative advocates telling him the same tired old platitudes in the same tired old circumstances. And he could scream.

Understand him. Sit there as you wait your turn and understand him. Feel what it must be like to have been sitting where he is for the last ten years. Feel the high ideals being eroded away by exasperation. Feel the conflict of duty and impatience. And if you feel this, really try to feel it, will you add to his afternoon's weight by some more turgid platitudes? Or will you make your points in as brief and businesslike fashion as you can, saying what you have to say as you might to a justifiably weary battle commander? Make his burden as sufferable as possible. Give it to him with brevity and sincerity and with regret that you have to trouble him. 'Sympathise' with him, for Goodness' sake! Be kind. Be helpful. He may just possibly notice it; he may feel a subconscious gratitude to you. If he does, then you have his sympathy. The drift has started. You have sympathised with him and as an almost inevitable consequence he has begun to sympathise with you. This is how it is done. It is totally honest: there is no trickery about it. If you give you will get back. Give sympathy and you will get sympathy.

So few advocates really think about this. If you do, you will be at a tremendous advantage. You may well appear to be the first person in the entire court building, apart from the usher, who seems real to the average juror. And if that is the case you will be listened to, not just heard.

It is therefore unnecessary to give you any hints on how to capture the sympathy of your audience. Techniques are almost self-defeating. But an illustration might help. Imagine how you would feel, sitting there on a jury, and one of the advocates says to the judge: 'My Lord, I have a point that I wish to raise in the absence of the jury.' What is your reaction? 'Absence of the jury? Why? What am I not being told? What does this fellow want to conceal from me and why does he want to conceal it? What's this all about?' But out you go to the jury-room. For ten minutes? Half an hour? The rest of the afternoon perhaps? The usher comes and says: 'The judge says you can go home. Come back by midday tomorrow'. 'Oh yes', you think, 'What are they getting up to in there? What am I not being permitted to know? What wool is being pulled over my eyes?'

So, so much easier it would have been if the lawyer had stood up and said:

'My Lord, there's a point of law that I must ask Your Lordship to decide upon. It's not going to concern the jury at all. Perhaps they could stretch their legs while we deal with it?'
'How long is it likely to take, Mr Snooks?'
'Well, frankly, My Lord, it could take the rest of the afternoon and perhaps even a bit of tomorrow morning. It's an awkward point of law. Your Lordship may even think it proper to suggest that the jury don't come back in until midday.'

Now *that* advocate isn't trying to conceal anything from you. He's asking the judge to give you a holiday. He's trying to fix a lie-in for you or the chance to get to the shops and the laundrette. No wool being pulled over your eyes here. Right?

Of course it's right. On the other hand, you may very well ask yourself, is this the first example we've come to in the book of lawyers' trickery at work? In a word, is it honest? Well, think about it. It is a matter of some importance, and it is worth taking a page or two to deal with it now, because the question of honesty and dishonesty in advocacy is a question that troubles most laymen and a lot of beginners in the legal profession.

The ethics of advocacy

The public attitude towards lawyers is both unfortunate and understandable. 'All lawyers are liars' is a very, very old adage. 'The first thing we do, we kill all the lawyers!' is another one, quoted, I think, rather than coined, by Shakespeare. We are thought to be capable of being purchased, willing to say anything and to espouse any cause provided the price is right. We are resented as well, and it is not hard to see why. If a plaintiff takes his case to court and wins, then he has

got only what justice demanded. Why should he have to pay a lawyer
to get what was his right anyway? If he loses, it is even worse. He put
out all those legal fees and he's got nothing to show for it. Either way
he feels resentful. And who can blame him? The layman also thinks
that the law is far too complicated and for that he blames the lawyers.
It is commonly believed that, as a profession, we make the law as
arcane as we can, intentionally designing things so that the layman will
not understand and will have to pay us to pilot him through the shoals
and sandbanks that we have schemingly laid down for his confusion
and our profit.

The fact that this is rubbish is almost irrelevant. The fact that the
lawyers do not make the law, but that Parliament and the judges are
responsible for that is equally irrelevant. The fact that the law is
inevitably a very complicated thing, as every law student knows only
too well, is again irrelevant. The lay public resent and mistrust us and
it is not difficult to sympathise with them. Apart from anything else we
don't try very much, as a profession, to do anything about it. We tend
to stand rather aloof when it comes to thinking about our public image
and despite the fact that there are many associations and committees
devoted to law reform, the legal professions don't accomplish much
when it comes to changing or improving the law. If you read the rules
of the American Bar Association you will find that there are two
professional requirements set out there that have no parallel in the
English codes of conduct. First, the American lawyer is required as a
matter of professional ethics to report gross incompetence on the part
of a brother lawyer. Whether that ever gets done is open to question,
but the point is that the requirement is written into the rules. There is
nothing like that in England. We have all been brought up never to
'split' on anybody. Second, the American lawyer has a professional
obligation to try at all times to improve the law itself. Again, in
England there is no such requirement. Yet the layperson's feeling
persists that we lawyers are to blame for the complexity of the law,
and that we are none of us really much better than hired guns willing
to do anything for a price.

There are two questions that barristers get asked over and over again
at cocktail parties, once it has got out that they are barristers. The
superficial one is: 'Ooh! Do you wear one of those funny sort of things
on your head?' That tends to be a bit less common than the other one.

'Tell me,' says your inquirer gravely, and you can hear it coming: again and again you can hear it coming. 'How can you defend a man you *know* is guilty?' You'd better work out your answer to that one early on, then commit it to memory, because you will encounter it again and again and again. You will find throughout your professional life that you are repeatedly having to explain to the layperson how it is that you can be a lawyer and at the same time an honest person. For this reason alone, it seems sensible to deal in this book, and at this early point, with some of the ethics of advocacy, with the honesty of the trade. One can hardly do more than touch upon it, for it is something that you will imbibe during pupillage and during your early years; but some of the most obvious things can be stated.

First, what *is* the answer to the question 'How can you defend a man you know is guilty?' It has been answered by all manner of famous men. I am not going to quote, however, but instead seek to answer it as most advocates today would probably answer it. And the answer is this: unless your client actually *tells* you that he is guilty, you do not *know* whether he is guilty or not. Oh, you have an opinion all right. Your *opinion* may be that he is as guilty as sin; but that's your opinion, not your knowledge. Suppose, therefore, that you think to yourself, 'The fellow is in my opinion clearly guilty: I'm not going to defend a guilty man', and you return the brief. He goes to another advocate. The other thinks exactly the same and he too refuses the case. On goes the guilty defendant to the next, and to the next and the next after that. The place where he is to be declared guilty is the court where there is a judge and a jury, both of whom have the task of deciding on guilt or innocence.

Yet as our defendant goes wearily from lawyer to lawyer, rapidly running through the legal profession, he has encountered condemnation after condemnation. Ultimately, he turns up in court quite unable to find anyone who will speak for him, who will use legal skill and experience to test the strength of the evidence of guilt, who will probe and explore on his behalf to find out whether things really are as they seem to be. He will be alone, unskilled and unhelped. Yet as anyone of a few years' experience will tell you, the evidence that points to apparent guilt has a strange habit of disintegrating time and time again in the law courts. Honestly directed cross-examination very frequently destroys the value of the accusation and demonstrates sometimes that the accused is anything but guilty. After a year or two in the courts you will have seen for yourself that things are often very different from what they appeared to be, and you will learn to be very chary in coming to an opinion on the guilt or innocence of anybody until you have seen and heard the witnesses. You will then understand the important difference between knowing that your client is guilty and having your private opinion that he is. You will also, in all probability, have encountered cases where you began privately convinced of your client's guilt and ended up acknowledging to yourself that you were plain wrong.

Because the Bar as a whole has seen, over the centuries, how mistaken an individual and initial impression can be, and because as a profession we abhor the thought that an accused person might find himself standing in the dock with no one to defend him, we have a thing called the 'cab-rank rule'. This means that providing a barrister is available to take the case and providing it is within his field of expertise and the fee is reasonable, then he *must* take the brief. If he refuses, he can be hauled up before the Professional Conduct Committee and disciplined for his refusal. If he privately thinks that his client is guilty, that is of no consequence. He is an advocate, not a judge. How — indeed, whether — the cab-rank rule will apply to solicitors, incidentally, remains to be seen.

If, on the other hand, your client tells you that he actually did what he is accused of but that he wishes to deny it in court, not only may you decline to appear for him: you must, subject to one reservation, return the brief. You are said at that point to be 'professionally embarrassed'. The reservation is this: if the client tells you that he is guilty but still wishes to defend the case you are entitled to test the evidence in cross-examination and to see whether it adds up to enough proof to show guilt; and you are entitled to submit to the judge that it does not. If the judge rules that there is enough of a case to go to the jury and to be decided by them, you are entitled to address the jury and to suggest that on this evidence they ought not to convict. But that is all. You are not allowed to put any questions in cross-examination that even suggest that your client is not guilty, nor are you permitted to put him into the witness box and let him testify that he did not do it. This is the only situation in which you may defend a man whom you know to be guilty. You are entitled, in fact, to find out whether his guilt can be *proved* according to law. If it cannot be, then it is in a sense in the public interest that he should be acquitted, since the bringing of cases on inadequate evidence is clearly to be discouraged. Even more important is it to make sure that there should be no *convictions* on inadequate evidence for if we permit that to happen, then nobody in this country is safe against wrongful accusation.

We go on evidence in our courts and the quality of the evidence should always be tested. That is one of the most important tasks of the advocate. We try to avoid prejudice of all kinds and we equally try to avoid any form of distortion. We are, strangely, not always concerned with getting at the truth. We are engaged, rather, in finding out whether a given body of evidence points to one result or the other, and if you think about it, that is how it should be, for, unless we go on the evidence, what can we go on?

Another illustration of the ethics of the Bar is this: if you are arguing a point of law before the judge and you know that there is a reported decision which is against you, then it is your duty to bring that decision to the attention both of the judge and of your opponent. If you fail to do that you are being dishonest, and if you acquire a reputation for tricky conduct, the Bar will brand you indelibly. You will never live it down.

No barrister will suggest a line of defence to his client. He may well tell his client that the defence being put up is simply not credible, but he will never suggest an alternative. Likewise no barrister will ever tell a witness what to say or how to say it. This, at least, *used* to be the rule, and at the time of writing things are in a certain state of flux. Because witness statements, 'proofs of evidence,' are now being used so frequently as a substitute for examination in chief in civil cases, both solicitors *and* barristers are now becoming involved in the drafting of such statements. In commercial cases, and where the client can afford to pay for a great deal of lawyering, witness statements are going through many drafts, being 'polished' — perhaps even 'massaged' — by lawyers. The lawyers are therefore *bound* to influence the way the witnesses express themselves. The ethical position, however, remains the same.

Misleading evidence

So let us come back to that point where we sent the jury away feeling that we were concealing something from them. We *were* concealing something from them. We were concealing the fact that there was evidence about to be called that might be very damaging indeed to our client's interests, yet we kept this fact from them and sent them away in such a manner as prevented them from even suspecting that something was going on behind their backs. How does this square up with the kind of honest dealing that we have been considering for the last few pages?

Well, you spent quite a bit of time studying the law of evidence and you discovered that a good deal of the case law of that subject was forged by the very highest appeal courts. What were they seeking to do, those top judges, when they strove to define the rules of evidence? Were they not trying to devise rules and guidelines that would separate out evidence which was reliable from that which was unreliable? In simplest terms that is what the law of evidence is about. We are concerned in a trial to get the right result. Anything other than that is a failure of the entire process, and worse than a waste of time and money: the wrong result is a messy failure called a 'miscarriage of justice'. One of the ways in which we seek to avoid that failure is to filter the available evidence. Over the centuries we have arrived at a series of processes for sorting out evidence into two piles — that which is helpful and that which, for one of countless different reasons, may be misleading. If the misleading evidence goes before the jury then their task is being made more difficult than it already is, and it is advocates' business to sort out with the judge whether or not evidence ought to go before the jury. If, in doing that, he clumsily leads the jury to believe that the wool may be being pulled over their eyes he can hardly be said to be making their task any easier. He runs the risk of complicating matters for them. Some bits of evidence *prove* very little indeed yet the effect that they can have on a group of people who are *feeling* as much as they are thinking may be to raise a suspicion that they simply cannot ignore. A baseless rumour can turn a crowd into a mob.

Accordingly, in borderline cases, it is only right that the experts should think carefully about the value of the evidence, and if there is doubt about it should thrash the matter out and decide whether it is likely, in accordance with the rules, to help the jury or to hinder them in coming to a proper result. So, you may feel, the lawyer who lets it be thought by the jury that something they might find interesting is being kept from them cannot be contributing to a proper outcome. There is concealment, but it is anything but dishonest.

This theme of honest dealing you will find recurring through this book, and as you gain experience in the courts you will see it in operation all the time. Look for it at all times; discover by watching and by asking what you may or may not do. Keep as your touchstone the fact that advocacy is at base all about straight dealing and remember that a lawyer caught out in a lie will almost certainly be booted out of the profession. Keep this in mind from the very outset and you will find pleasure in discovering what an utterly honourable profession that of an advocate is.

Those, then, are the four quite basic rules of advocacy. First, decide whom you are talking to and adjust your language and approach to your audience. Second, strive to keep the interest of your audience. Third, be as kind as you can at all times. Fourth, aim from the outset to capture and keep the sympathy of your audience. All other rules are in a sense either subdivisions or elaborations upon those four fundamental aspirations. Aim for those four and a lot will take care of itself. Let us come now to a handful of specific hints and warnings.

Hints and warnings

Let us begin with a warning. *Never throw down a gauntlet to a jury.* Advocates are still heard to say, 'You can't convict, Members of the Jury!' and you can watch the indefinable change that comes over the composite animal as twelve minds in unison say silently to themselves, 'Oh, yes, we can!' In advocacy, as in physics, every action has its equal and opposite reaction. Throw down a challenge and it will be taken up, you can be sure of that.

> 'You couldn't possibly. . . 'Couldn't we now?'
> 'You won't . . .' 'Oh won't we?'

If you remember that you are supposed to be 'feeling along with' the jury you will just not be able to challenge them in this way. This is because a challenge involves two sides. If you remember that you ought to be with them, on the same wavelength as them, how then should you express that thought, 'You can't convict my client'? Might it not be something like this?

If the evidence has pushed you into a position where you feel that you have no choice except to convict John Smith then you'll have to do just that. But has the evidence pushed you into that position? I'd suggest it's done nothing of the kind. Far from it. On this evidence you have been left quite free to acquit, and you may find yourselves feeling that you just can't convict. (Tiny pause) It's for you to decide.

Now let us analyse some of the ideas and phrases that go to make up that little paragraph.

(a)   'If the evidence has pushed you into a position . . .'. No one likes to be pushed into any position. They prefer to be free. But the whole basis on which our system of criminal justice is grounded is that there should only be a conviction when the evidence makes it impossible sensibly to acquit, which is the same as saying when the jury has indeed been left with no reasonable alternative. They may be led into the position of having no choice, but the semantics of whether they have been led or have been pushed involve hair-splitting. If you suggest to the jury that they have been pushed into something it is a perfectly honest suggestion: they *should* be pushed by the evidence if they are going to convict. And yet the phrase 'being pushed' is useful to you as an advocate. Suggest that they have been pushed into something and their equal and opposite reaction will be to say, 'Oh, have we now?'

(b)   'I'd suggest it's done nothing of the kind.' Here you are identifying with their 'Oh, have we now?' They are not inclined to be pushed anywhere, and here are you agreeing with them. You are saying what they think. You are in sympathy with them and, so it tends to follow, they are in sympathy with you.

(c)   'On this evidence you have been left quite free to acquit.' Their response must be something like, 'So we have. We *have* been left quite free. We are not going to be pushed into anything.' And again you are taking them with you and going with them. You are keeping their sympathy. You are understanding your audience.

(d)   'And you may find yourself feeling that you just can't convict.' There you are: you've used the very words, but *you prepared the way,* you led their minds to the idea through a thicket of equal and opposite reactions. And notice the words, 'You may find yourself feeling'. Those words are tentative, they push nobody, they attract no equal and opposite reactions. If you say, 'You feel this, don't you?', you risk the answer 'No'. But if you use the bland 'You may find yourselves feeling' you risk nothing of the kind. It is not so much a suggestion as a mere observation, yet it brings you effortlessly to what you wanted to say in the first place: 'You cannot convict!'

(e)   'It's for you to decide.' This is both a safety net and at the same time a buttress for what you've already been doing. As a buttress it reminds the jury that you are not trying to push them anywhere. As a safety net it protects you against any slight challenge that the use of the words 'you can't convict' may perhaps have risked raising.

Never raise your voice.   Keep this simple rule in mind at all times. You will soon learn when you encounter one of those very rare situations where you can break the rule. The inexperienced speaker tends not to know this. He thinks that by raising his voice he emphasises his point. But it doesn't work. If you raise your voice you become immediately suspect and even the sleepiest juror will suddenly wonder what has happened to you. Even if you change your tone by a minuscule amount it will be noticed, and the same goes for your pace of delivery. That's all right. But if you raise your voice it will appear that you have somehow lost control of the situation and your credibility will at once be in doubt. Why this should be the case is very difficult to define, but as a rule it's almost inflexible.

Know what your face is doing.   You have already been cautioned about this. Give nothing away by your facial expressions that you do

not intend to give away. With some people this is easy. They have the kind of faces that do not flash signals all about them. Others have such mobile faces that they are flashing unintended signals all the time. Look around you in a crowded student bar and you will see exactly what I mean. It's up to you to find out which kind of face you've got. If you are a signal-flasher then you are going to have to learn to control it.

There is also another aspect to this face business. Some people signal very little while they are silent but as soon as they start to talk, especially if they are under any kind of pressure, they twist their faces up into strange expressions. The frown is the commonest manifestation

of this, and the habit can be very distracting to your audience. I was judging a moot some time ago. Before me was an excellent student who knew his case law perfectly and whose manner of delivery was very good indeed. His team won and deservedly so. The trouble was that whenever he opened his mouth to speak he contorted his face into the most piteous, cringing sort of frown. When he stopped talking he relaxed into a quite pleasant normality. But it got to the point where I was watching, fascinated, rather than listening properly to what he had to say. I was really distracted. If he comes to the Bar somebody is going to have to take him aside and tell him about it because his present habit is going to irritate both judge and jury. And, of course, it isn't something that one normally feels comfortable mentioning to somebody. That is why I am dwelling on it here. What you should do is to be aware of the muscles of your face and discover what they do. Try to find out whether you have an unintended sneer, or an unhappy little frown that you hitherto knew nothing about, or a propensity to any kind of extreme. If you have, then work to control it. You will pick up a great deal of feedback from the faces of witnesses and jurors and even judges. You must know what it is that you, via your face, are putting out. Do understand, you are not being encouraged to learn some kind of facial semaphore so that you can wave flags at the jury. You are being urged to know your face so that you can avoid waving those flags. Don't feel silly or shy about considering this aspect of yourself. It matters.

Aim to be the honest guide.   This involves two things and they are equally important. First, you have got to be trusted by the jury. They must be made to feel from the outset, or from as near to the outset as you can contrive it, to feel that you are fair and honest — trustworthy, in a word. Second, you have got to aim from the earliest possible moment to let them see where you are going. As was said earlier, all these dos and don'ts are only elaborations upon the four basic rules, and the 'honest guide' rule is simply an extension of the 'sympathy' rule. Let us take these two points separately.

You have got to be trusted.   By following the basic rules you will automatically incline the jury to trust you. What you must aim for is to avoid disturbing that trust. And the worst pitfall that you may encounter here is misquoting the evidence. Let me explain. When the evidence has all been called you will address the jury on its value. If you say that witness X testified to so and so when in fact he said something different you are almost lost. You may be corrected by the judge, which might make you look foolish or even dishonest. Worse, the jury may recognise the difference for themselves and suddenly they are no longer with you. This may also occur when you are examining or cross-examining a witness. You sometimes have to 'put' to a witness what a previous witness has said. If you get it wrong then both judge and jury may well notice it and, again, you are in deep trouble.

All of which indicates the overwhelming need for accuracy on your part. A careless slip can obliterate your credibility and an innocent mistake can start the court wondering if you might be dishonest. Realise this and realise the enormous importance of taking an accurate note. There is a section elsewhere in this book about note-taking and all that needs to be said here is that you should *never* refer to specific evidence unless you are sure that you know exactly what that evidence was. You get it wrong at your peril.

What do you do if you fall into this trap? Can you extricate yourself? You may be able to, but it can only be done by a little honest self-abasement. If the judge corrects you, you pause, and if you *are* a little puzzled, you are entitled to appear to be. Then you say something like, 'My Lord, I'm sorry. I must have completely misunderstood what the witness said. I'm grateful to Your Lordship. The last thing I want to do is to take a false point.' It must be said with gravity and sincerity and everything about your tone and your expression must indicate that you *are glad* to have been corrected. If you happen to have been addressing the jury when the judge corrected you, you can restart with them by some such words as: 'Well, Members of the Jury, I'm sorry to have wasted your time. Let me turn to something quite different.'

Bear in mind that we all make mistakes. And remember that the best way of repairing your position is to be openly honest and unhesitatingly apologetic. Anyone who says, 'I'm sorry' usually attracts the equal and opposite, 'That's all right'; and moving on quickly to something else quickly closes the incident. Bear in mind, too, that handling your mistakes in the right way can make you more human in the jury's eyes and increase the sympathy between you. Take, for instance, the error that most of us fall into, some more often than others, of starting a sentence and getting lost half way. There you are, surrounded by subordinate clauses and parentheses, you've forgotten where you were going and you are well and truly lost. The inexperienced often feel that they have no alternative but to plough on, and so the mess gets worse, the advocate feels flustered, it shows in his face or in his tone of voice and the jury start losing the drift, finding that the hitherto entertaining programme is suddenly boring. What does the experienced advocate do? He quickly realises that his sentence is a failure and he stops dead in his tracks. He abandons it, brushes it off with the rapid and matter-of-fact words, 'Let me start that sentence again'. And on he goes. It has done him no harm at all. Before he even began to lose the jury's attention he in fact took a closer hold on it. He has made himself more human in their eyes, more like them, and he has given himself a totally fresh start. He could have said alternatively: 'No. That's not how I want to put it. Let me begin again'; or: 'I feel I'm not putting this as clearly as I'd like to, Members of the Jury. Let me try to put it another way.' By such honest observations that you are not content with your own efforts you are likely to attract the equal and opposite reaction of the jury which will be the unspoken thought: 'No, no. Go on. You're not doing badly at all.'

It is not being suggested that you should pepper your speeches with apologies for your inadequacies. If you say, 'Let me start that sentence again' more than a few times in any speech it will start to stick out like a mannerism. What is being suggested is that when you do make a mistake you put it right as quickly as possible by acknowledgement of the fact. The time to attempt to conceal your mistakes is in the examination of witnesses and we will come to that later.

The other way in which you risk losing the trust of the jury is by suggesting to them things that they simply cannot accept. If the evidence does not add up to a result that is credible, do not lose *your* credibility by suggesting that it does. If the evidence does point clearly in one direction only, don't insult their collective intelligence by suggesting that it doesn't. Do not suggest to them that they can walk through a brick wall because they know that they cannot. Direct your efforts instead to showing them how they might get round it or over it. In a word, do not take false points.

Likewise, do not make unfair points. This is at least as important as not taking false points. The points that you make must *feel* honest to the jury. If you are in sympathy with them you ought to feel what they will regard as fair or unfair. Some really gutter advocates take the attitude that if the witness is a detective of the Metropolitan Police then he is lying, and they are foolish enough to address the jury on that basis. This approach hardly ever succeeds. Apart from its barbarity, it displays a total lack of sympathy with the jury's prejudices, and it seems what it is: unfair. In truth there are police witnesses who lie. Defending advocates find that there are occasions when their entire case depends on attempting to demonstrate that the police witnesses are lying. And the unfortunate fact is that in Her Majesty's prisons are a number of ex-policemen who did lie in court. There are a host of honest policemen as well.

But, if one does have to suggest police dishonesty to a jury, it has to be suggested in a way which is seen and felt to be fair. Like this, for instance:

One unhappy thing about this case is that I've had to suggest that the police have been deceiving us. It's not a pretty thought, is it, Members of the Jury? It's not something that any of us want to admit, the thought that the police who look after this city of ours and who make it safe for us to sleep at night might have among them policemen who are willing to lie to judge and jury so as to get somebody convicted, policemen who are prepared to stretch and bend the law. It's frightening, is it not? We'd rather not think about it: we wish it wasn't true. We'd like to turn our backs on such an idea as we turn away from other nasty thoughts. But, unfortunately, we can't do that. Unfortunately, we can't live in this country today without knowing that it *can* happen. Everything in us says, 'No. I don't want to believe it', but we know perfectly well that it happens and we have the unsavoury task of answering the unpleasant question — did it happen in this case? Because if it did, and if this defendant is convicted, then the wool will have been pulled over everybody's eyes and we will all have played our part in what is called a miscarriage of justice. So we can't start off just assuming that these police witnesses are honest. If you did that, you'd be failing in your duty. If you accept their evidence, you have to be able to feel that there is good reason for accepting it. Unfortunately, we can no longer say, as we used to be able to say: they are policemen, so they must be telling the truth. It's a pity, but that's no longer enough. So let's look to see what quality evidence we've got in this case. Let's think what evidence you'd like to have had, what evidence you might expect to have had, what evidence you could very easily have had; and let's see what evidence you've actually got. Because it's on the evidence that you've got, that you are going to tell us if this accused person is to be convicted or acquitted.

Now does that feel fair? I hope so. You will generally find that an objective standard of fair play and fair thinking is present in a jury from first to last. Never abuse that. It is probably the jury's greatest strength.

Let them know as best you can exactly where you are going. This is the second limb of the rule that you should always appear to be the honest guide. This part of the rule is difficult to accomplish in practice and it is difficult to advise you about in theory. But the principle can be explained and you can keep it in mind as one of your objectives. You should begin by assuming that everything is unfamiliar to the juror. She is a stranger to the court building and even more so to the court-room. Don't forget that many people are actually afraid of courts in the same way as they are afraid of hospitals and dentists' surgeries. They feel nervous as they come through the main door and they remain nervous and jumpy for quite a while. Travel up in the lift at the Old Bailey on a Monday morning with a crowd of new jurors and you will find most of them silent and bemused with one or two talking breezily to cover their uncertainty. The same jurors three days later will be behaving quite differently, treating the place as if they are a part of it, as indeed they are.

The stint of jury service usually means that one juror will sit success-ively on more than one case and it is good sense to inquire of your usher whether you have a 'new' jury or not. If they are 'new' you *must* treat them as being unfamiliar and unaware. If they are not, you can adjust your approach accordingly. An example: when, as defence counsel, you address them at the end of the trial you must deal with the burden of proof and the standard of proof (of which more later). If they are an experienced jury they will almost certainly have heard about it before and if you don't take account of that you may do yourself less than justice. It is about as important a part as any of the defender's tasks to make sure that the jury really understand the burden of proof, and as you get ready to begin on that topic you really ought to know if you are bringing them a brand new concept or if it is something already familiar to them. You cannot have them thinking as you start, 'Here we go again'. So with an experienced jury you have to introduce your observations with words which acknowledge that you are about to deal with something that you know they are already familiar with. Perhaps thus:

> Now if, as I think is the case, you, ladies and gentlemen, have already sat on a jury in another trial what I'm about to say will be familiar to you. But it is *so* important that I would be quite failing in my duty if I did not talk to you about it. It is so important that if I missed it out or passed quickly over it I would just not be doing my job properly. So I know you will all bear with me. You may even find that I deal with it a bit differently from other people that you've listened to.

By such words, or others like them, you totally avoid the jury's thinking 'Oh dear, not that again!' On the contrary, you have (i) twice emphasised before even starting how important the topic is; (ii) asked them to bear with you, which tips your hat to the sympathy rule; and (iii) hinted that your version may be different from others they have heard, which is in accordance with the 'keep their interest' rule.

Even if they have done a case or two and so have learned some of the ropes — which juries do very quickly — a new case is still very much uncharted territory as far as they are concerned. So (and here we come to the second limb of the 'honest guide' rule) try from the earliest possible moment to make clear what your line is. With some defending advocates one finds that one is two or three days into the case and one still doesn't know where they are going or what they are seeking to prove. With others one knows it almost from the beginning. Try to do this. Take every legitimate opportunity you can to clarify your position. Try, early in your first cross-examination, to let them see what you are driving at. The sooner you begin to remove the mystery the sooner you will have their sympathy. Comment, as such, is not permitted until that stage in the trial when the rules allow it, so you cannot declare your position in a series of preambles to your questions in cross-examination. You can quite legitimately, however, seek to show where you are going by the *occasional* short preamble to a question. Generally speaking, however, if you frame your questions properly there should be very little temptation to comment. Your drift should become quite clear.

If by your fourth cross-examination the jury do not have a pretty fair idea of your case then you are not doing it properly. You must aim from the outset to take them along with you and unless you show them where you are going they cannot be blamed if they do not want to come. Bear in mind that you can accomplish quite a lot by making admissions at the end of the prosecutor's opening speech. He will wind up with some such words as, 'And now, with His Lordship's leave, I shall call the evidence before you'. At this point you can rise to your feet.

'My Lord', you say, 'I hope Your Lordship and my friend will forgive me, but I may be able to save everybody's time if I say that there is no dispute that Mr X had property stolen from him on the night of the

16th June. The defendant's case being that he was in no way involved, he cannot dispute that there was indeed a theft. I am willing therefore to make a formal admission that the theft took place because since the defendant knows nothing about it one way or the other, I cannot challenge it.' Say it crisply, clearly and in as friendly a manner as you can. A reasonable judge will not complain if you say that. An awkward judge might barge in and accuse you of making a speech. If he does, apologise. Say: 'I'm sorry, My Lord. I was seeking to save Your Lordship's time and make it easier for the jury.' If the judge is so rude as to barrack you at that point, say, 'So be it, My Lord', and sit down. You will have made it clear to anyone in that court-room who may be interested the direction in which you are going.

(Formal admissions, incidentally, are a very useful method of putting unchallenged, or agreed, evidence before a jury. Much time can be saved, as can be seen in the above illustration. However, the form of the admission can vary. Often the evidence it contains is very simple and can be stated in one short sentence. In complicated cases, however, one may find a formal admission stretching to many paragraphs. In such circumstances, the formal admission should be reduced to writing; indeed, the Court of Appeal has ruled that all formal admissions be so reduced. However, it is not uncommon to see very simple formal admissions being made orally; remember, the judge will himself take a note of the admission for the purposes of summing up.)

Maintain your status.   This can be dealt with very shortly. The jury will not find for your client because they like you. They will, however, listen with greater attention and more sympathy to what you have to say. And since you, as advocate, are your client's voice, you are doing nothing more than your duty by him if you work hard to maintain the ear of the jury. Try, therefore, to avoid conflicts with the judge. If he smacks you down, you may lose face in the eyes of the jury. It takes quite a bit of experience to be able to stand up to a judge. At the outset of your career accept the difficult judge as one of the shortcomings of our system. Keep your cool and back off with as much dignity as you can muster. Strive not to appear to wilt or cower. The judge is in charge. Take what he dishes out. Keep cool and *always* say, as you sit down, 'If Your Lordship pleases'. At least it gives you the last word and goes some way to evening up the balance. One cannot leave this bit of advice without mentioning the concept of 'riding the bumps', but we will deal with that when we come to discuss cross-examination.

Make a point of looking at the jury. This is essential. You cannot communicate with people who are in your company unless you look at them. Don't overdo it, but don't ignore them either. It is only from what you see on their faces that you can get any idea of how they are listening and of how they are receiving your efforts and that of the others in the court. When they come into the jury box for the first time watch them individually. Do not fix them with a pebble stare but watch each juror as you might watch a prize winner at school going to collect her prize. Look interested — you ought to *be* interested. By this time you should know what your face is or is not signalling. You ought to be and ought to appear to be one of the people in court that the juror would feel comfortable about approaching and asking help from. As they come into the jury box they are being watched intently by the clerk of the court. The judge not infrequently ignores them altogether. So do the other lawyers. If the juror sees one apparently interested and sympathetic onlooker — and you ought to be both — he or she may think that you at least 'feel' comfortable. If that is the case, you and that juror have begun that exchange of sympathy that will help your cause throughout the trial. The kindness that ought to flow throughout the proceedings will genuinely have been put into effect. You will have begun properly.

During the trial be careful not to roll your eyes and shrug your shoulders at the jury. No kind of gross sucking up to them is proper. But do please remember that the questions you ask are designed not to bring information before you but before *them*. In one sense you are asking questions on their behalf, and if you do not glance at them as you obtain significant answers you will not be able to tell whether they appear to be grasping that significance. There is perhaps, one time when you do not look at the jury, and that is when they come back into court after deliberating their verdict. While you wait for that verdict keep your eyes fixed firmly on the papers in front of you. It is, if you think about it, a simple matter of courtesy, since, if as is to be hoped, they have come to like you, they may very well feel faintly embarrassed at having to disappoint you by finding against you.

An odd rule of professional conduct in England says that an advocate ought to avoid contact with his jurors after the trial is over. In some ways this is a pity because one never knows what the jury were impressed by, what they found helpful, what they felt they had to disregard. And since an advocate will never get the chance of sitting on a jury he will never have any real idea of what goes on in the minds of the people that he has devoted all his skills to. In some states in America it is regarded as professional misconduct *not* to interview the jurors after the trial. Perhaps some half-way house would be ideal. Apart from anything else one tends to feel, during a longish trial, that one has got to know one's jurors pretty well and a lot of us feel that it would be agreeable at least to chat briefly with them after the trial is over. Still, as so many of our judges say, there it is.

Four

The client's character

By way of introduction let us first have a look at another fairly basic rule: *try to work out what are all the weak points in your case and try to get to them before anyone else does.* Every case has weak points. If *you* deal with them as soon as possible, it is far, far better than letting your opponent spring them on the court. You cannot, of course, hope to do this with all your weak points, but aim to do it at all times. Likewise, if you know what those weak points are you can aim to prepare the jury for them. Always be honest — this cannot be emphasised too much. If you can possibly play all your cards completely face up, do so. If you can do this then you can tell the jury that you have done so, and if you are doing your job properly they will see that this is so.

For this reason always give real thought, in a criminal case, to whether you can put your client's 'character' before the jury. As you know, the general rule is that the previous convictions of an accused person are not to be put in evidence. This is because it is felt that a jury may well think, if they know that they are dealing with an habitual law-breaker, that he is more likely to have committed the offence than a person who had never offended before. If the accused attacks the honesty of prosecution witnesses, of course, then, if he chooses to give evidence, it is thought proper for the jury to know what kind of person is making this attack; and on the prosecutor's application the judge may well allow cross-examination of the accused on his previous character and evidence of previous convictions to be given.

Now a good advocate will never let things get to the stage where his opponent makes such an application, let alone where the judge grants it. The good advocate will have realised early in his preparing of the case whether he will have to attack a prosecution witness's integrity,

and he will have explained to his client that such an attack will almost
certainly lead to the 'character' of the accused 'going in'. He will have
decided before the trial begins whether his client's character is going
to have to be put before the jury, and if it is, then *he* will put that
character in evidence. At the earliest possible stage in the earliest
appropriate cross-examination of a police officer he will say something
like:

> 'Now, officer, I want the ladies and gentlemen of the jury to know
> exactly what kind of person it is they are trying. Would you be kind
> enough to have before you the antecedents in respect of William
> Sykes?' The officer in charge of the case will probably be sitting in
> court, will produce the document and hand it to the usher who will
> in turn pass it to the witness. As this is being done say to the judge:
> 'I don't know if Your Lordship has a copy?'
> 'No, Mr Snooks.'
> 'Well, I think it would assist Your Lordship to have the record before
> you.' (. . . and turn to where the officer is getting papers from his
> file . . .) 'A copy for My Lord, please, usher.'

Make it business-like. Make it look as if it is your positive wish that
judge and jury should know all about your client's previous villainy.
If you make a virtue out of necessity and do it properly you will
frequently find that at least half the damage that might otherwise be
done to your cause simply goes away.

You must previously have been through your client's background with
a fine-tooth comb. You should have checked with him personally, in
conference, every entry on his criminal record and any short summaries
produced by the police of such previous convictions. You will have
asked him about every offence recorded against him, about the facts
that gave rise to them, about any extenuating circumstances and about
two other vital things: (a) did he have the services of a lawyer at the
court where he appeared; and (b) did he plead guilty or not guilty? It
is astonishing how many defendants with a record of a dozen or more
previous convictions pleaded guilty to every offence that they had ever
been charged with. If you find that this is the case then you are able to
say in utmost honesty at some later stage in the case, 'And, Members
of the Jury, you will not have missed the fact that this is the very first
time William Sykes has ever refused to admit being guilty as charged.

It is the first time that he has ever said to a court of law "I didn't do it: I am innocent of what they accuse me of." '

Make quite sure that this is in fact so before you say it. It would be carelessness amounting to dishonesty on your part if you said this when in fact your client had even been acquitted of a charge in the past. But if it is indeed the case that he has never before made a fight of it, do not pass by the chance of using this good jury point.

If, as is usually the case, the client *has* fought cases in the past and been convicted notwithstanding, then the point will probably be made by somebody sooner or later that he had, on that previous occasion, 'not been believed upon his oath'. Although theoretically disapproved of, it happens all the time and it will usually be said by the prosecutor in cross-examination of your client.

> 'Did you plead guilty or not guilty to that charge?'
> 'Not guilty.'
> 'Did you give evidence before a jury in that case?'
> 'Yes.'
> 'And you were convicted . . . that jury disbelieved you upon your oath?'
> 'Well, um . . .'
> 'Well, that must be right, must it not?'
> 'Well, um . . . Yes.'
> 'Yes. I see. Now how about the conviction for wounding in 1975? Did you plead guilty or not guilty to that charge?'

. . . and so on.

Do not let this happen. At least, do not let the prosecutor be the first to say it. When going through your client's character with the police witness, deal with the matter and use the very words yourself.

> 'The burglary in 1975, officer. Is it right that William Sykes pleaded not guilty to that charge?'
> 'I believe so, sir, yes.'
> 'Yet, he was convicted. The jury in that trial disbelieved him upon his oath?'
> 'Yes, sir.'

'And the same goes for the wounding in 1975?'
'Yes, sir.'
'He pleaded guilty, I think to the 1979 criminal damage matter?'
'Yes, sir.'

If it comes from you, clinically, smoothly, with you being totally unruffled and totally business-like about it, the jury will incline to the feeling that you clearly have things under control and that, despite all this awful past, there must be good reason for this case being contested, otherwise a sensible person like you would not be contesting it. If you let the facts come out through the prosecutor's questions then you not only lose that advantage but you also permit your opponent with legitimate tone-of-voice inflections, to imply that your client is a rogue and a vagabond.

In a word, go out and grasp every nettle you dare. Your client's character is just the most obvious example. Some advocates keep it out at all costs. Others feel that the advantage to be gained from grasping every nettle and later, being able to say to the jury in all honesty that nothing has been concealed from them, outweighs the disadvantage of the client's previous convictions being there in evidence. It's also worth remembering that a jury which has already tried one or two cases may well have 'twigged' that total silence as to the previous convictions of the accused almost certainly means he has some. This is another reason why it is often a good thing to grasp the nettle and put in your own client's 'bad' character.

Bear in mind that the usual witness to ask about your client's past is the 'officer in charge of the case'. He often gives evidence last. By asking the first available witness to deal with this matter you may ruffle the judge a bit. If he complains, say: 'I want the jury to know at the earliest possible time about this defendant's previous record, Your Honour, and I'd be grateful if you'd permit details to be given by this witness. They can be amplified later if necessary.' It takes a churlish judge to refuse that, and even if he does stop you and you have to say, 'So be it, Your Honour', you have still appeared to the jury as an honest guide.

Remember, too, that if you do grasp the nettle and put in your client's character you are entitled to put in the whole of his character. This is important. There may be all manner of mitigating circumstances along the way. Always note in advance how old he was when he committed the offences recorded. Ten years is not all that big a time space to a 45-year old, but the difference between someone aged 19 and the same person aged 29 can be enormous. Note whether there was a spate of offences just when, for instance, his wife left him or when, perhaps, his child was killed in a traffic accident. There *are* people in our society who are straight villains and you will certainly represent clients of whom virtually nothing good can be said. But they are surprisingly rare. There is usually in every history of convictions, a good deal of mitigating material. Make sure you know what that mitigating material is before ever the case begins, and if you put in the previous convictions of your client be sure to put before the jury the mitigating material at the same time. But great care must be taken to make sure that the extenuating material that you put before the jury when introducing your client's character is indeed real mitigation and not a schmaltzy string of cheap excuses. Make sure, too, that you introduce the mitigating features in as matter of fact a way as possible. An illustration:

Q He was convicted in July 1975, was he not, of armed robbery and sentenced to three years' imprisonment?

A Yes, sir.

Q He seems to have been 18 ½ years old at the time of that offence?

A Yes, about that, sir.

Q That would have been about a year after he came to this country from the place where he was born?

A It seems so, sir.

Q Is it right that the robbery was committed in the company of two others older than himself?

A Yes, sir.

Q A shop assistant was threatened with a knife and tied up, correct?

A Yes, sir.

Q And about £900 was stolen?

A £885, sir.

Q And Fagin was outside the shop keeping a look-out?

A Yes, sir.

Q He pleaded guilty, I think?

A That's right, sir.

Q Tell me, officer, when he came to this country did he have other members of his family with him or was he alone in England?

A   The records don't disclose, sir.

Q   They don't? Very well, officer. Thank you.

You have stuck strictly to cold fact there, yet the picture has quietly emerged of a lonely newcomer to this country who has fallen into bad company when at a pathetically impressionable age, and who has taken a minor part in comparatively petty robbery, being soundly punished for it despite the fact that he readily accepted his guilt. You have made no attempt to advance any excuse for his conduct, yet all the mitigation is there in evidence, and its effect is all the stronger because you offered it as fact and not as excuse. Just consider how the same facts could have been mishandled:

Q   He was very young when he was involved in that robbery, wasn't he, officer?

A   Depends what you call young, sir. He was 18½.

Q   Well, he hadn't been very long in this country either?

A   He'd been in England for about a year, sir.

Q   And wasn't he a very lonely young man at the time?

A   I really couldn't say, sir.

Q   And didn't he play a very minor part in that robbery, officer?

A   He was part of a team of three, sir. He was the look-out while his two associates threatened the shop assistant with a knife, tied her up and made off with going on for a thousand pounds. If you think that was a minor part that's a matter for you, sir.

Q   But he'd got into bad company, officer?

A   Oh yes, sir, I'd agree he'd got into bad company all right.

Point made? Stick to facts. Offer no excuses. But make sure that all those mitigating facts *do* emerge when leading evidence of your client's bad character. And realise, too, how vital it is that it should be you, not your opponent, who leads that evidence. Imagine how coldly he would deal with the same facts. Not one iota of mitigation would emerge then. Remember the rule: get to your weak points before anyone else does. Always aim for that.

Five

Three mandatory rules and some essential aims

1 Lay the foundation for any comments you intend to make. Now this is not so much advice that you are being offered. This is a mandatory rule that *must* be followed. What it amounts to is this. At the end of the case you will be making a speech to the jury or to your bench. In that speech you may make comments to them on the evidence and on the surrounding facts of the case. *You are not allowed to comment on matters which have not been touched upon during the evidence.* An illustration: take a case where the question of visibility arises. You may want to suggest that the visibility would have been greatly cut down if it had been raining at the relevant time. If the question has not been raised during the evidence as to whether it was raining or not, then you are not permitted to mention it in your closing speech. If you want to comment on it then you must make sure that the 'ground is laid' for your comment. This does not mean that you personally have to lay that ground. If your opponent, or one of your co-defenders has dealt with the matter so that it has been raised in evidence, then there is no need for you to deal with the matter further. But if the matter on which you want to comment is not raised by somebody else then you have to raise it yourself.

If you think about it, the rule is only a matter of common sense and fairness. You cannot properly raise a point for the first time in your final speech. If it had been raised earlier somebody might have wanted to ask questions about it, to investigate it further, perhaps even to call fresh evidence about it.

Go back to the visibility illustration. It has occurred to you that visibility would be reduced in given climatic conditions. You want to investigate it. You ask the first witness. He can't remember. You ask the second witness. He can't remember either. If you want to be able to comment in your final speech you must raise the matter with each witness who might be able to throw light on the subject. Only if you do this will you be able to turn to the jury and say, 'One of the odd things about the case is that nobody can remember one way or the other if it was raining at the time. It might have been, it might not. But if it *had* been raining, you may think that would have made it more difficult to see . . .' and so on.

Go back to character. If nothing has been said in the evidence about character you cannot later comment to the jury that so and so is of good character. No ground has been laid. There is no factual evidence upon which you can base your comment.

What is and what is not enough 'ground-laying' to justify a later comment is something that you will learn by experience and cannot be taught in a book. But bear in mind that a little can often be enough. As long as there is adequate evidence about a point you may comment on that point. Ask yourself this as a rule-of-thumb test: am I making a comment about which my opponent could say, 'Hold on, that's something you could have asked witness so and so about'? If you have explored the question and given the witnesses a fair opportunity to deal with the point, you may comment on it. The reason for this rule should by now be clear: in court we go on evidence and not on opinions. Like every regulation, there are exceptions even to this. Expert witnesses can give opinions, but in virtually all other instances witnesses give evidence as to facts and opinion is avoided. We work on the evidence and on the inferences that may be drawn from that evidence. That is why the 'ground must be laid' for comment. This brings us to the next point.

2   *Never, when acting as an advocate, give or appear to give evidence yourself.*   The proper place for evidence to come from is the witness box, not the Bar. Always remember this, and resist the temptation to say anything which smacks of giving evidence yourself. I once heard an excellent pupil, doing his first jury trial, and doing it very well, say to the jury in his final speech: 'And you know, Members of the Jury, over the lunch adjournment my client said to me . . .'. Until then he had been doing beautifully. And suddenly he branded himself a

complete newcomer to the job. He was giving evidence, blatantly and in all innocence. It was such a fundamental error that his pupil master had never even considered cautioning him against it.

That is a pretty extreme example and you will easily avoid that mistake if you know the rule. What is sometimes a bit more tricky is to avoid the semblance of giving evidence while you are questioning a witness. You *are* permitted to preface some of your questions with an explanation so as to shorten them or so as to clarify their meaning. An example. The defence advocate says: 'We have heard that the robber was wearing a light blue anorak. Do you recall that the person you saw running down the road was wearing that kind of garment?' Here you are *repeating* evidence, not giving it for the first time, and this is permissible. It would not be permissible if, for instance, you said: 'It was raining at the time, Mr Brown. Did you have your wipers on?' If there had not already been evidence that it was raining then you would be giving fresh evidence yourself. If there had, in fact, been evidence that it was raining then you would have been entitled to say: 'We have heard that it was raining. Do you agree?' And then, if the witness did agree, you could ask, 'Did you have your wipers on?'

In similar fashion, you would never say to a jury, 'I happen to be acquainted with this junction and I can tell you . . .'. Nobody is interested in whether you designed and built the junction with your bare hands: you are an advocate, not a witness. Likewise, you must avoid saying: 'As you may very well know, Members of the Jury, there is a direct rail-link between X and Y'. They may indeed know it: they may not. In either event you should not say it because you are giving evidence if you do. If the matter is relevant then you should have brought it out in the evidence of some witness during the trial. If you did not do this, do not make the comment.

You may well be wondering whether there are some facts which are so well known that they can be referred to without actually having been led in evidence. The answer is yes, of course there are. You don't need to adduce evidence during the trial that the M1 is a motorway connecting London and the North of England. You may refer to such an obvious fact without actually establishing it in the evidence. But if you want to refer to the fact that the M1 runs near to Northampton then even though everyone in court may know the fact, you ought not to refer to it unless there is a basis of evidence to that effect. What is and what is not *such* common knowledge as not to require proof is a question of judgment. It is probably safe to assume that the whole of the population of England know that there is a television programme called 'Coronation Street' and you could probably make mention of that fact without offending against the 'no evidence from the advocate' rule. But to assert on which day or days Coronation Street is broadcast would be improper. The basic rule, 'If in doubt, don't', is applicable here as in most stages of advocacy. If what you are about to say could offend against the 'no evidence rule' then find some other way of doing it. Just as important as the 'no evidence rule' is the last of the three mandatory rules.

3 The advocate's opinion is not evidence and it is certainly not relevant.   For this reason you never tell the jury what you personally think about evidence, or about anything else for that matter. You leave it to them to form opinions and to reach conclusions. Never may you tell them how it seems to you, how you react to a piece of evidence. You never even hint at what you think or feel by saying anything that can be read as you personally expressing a view.

But, you may say, if the advocate doesn't appear to believe in his case, doesn't he weaken his position and do a grave disservice to his client? Of course he does. He ought always to convey as much confidence in his cause as reasonableness permits. He must, if he can, make the jury feel that he is totally convinced of his case. But he must not *tell* them that, in terms. He has to convey it in other ways, and this is why English advocates tend to use phrases which are not to be found in everyday parlance. How is it done? How may one persuade a jury while at the same time voicing no opinion whatsoever?

It is done by a series of phrases which ensure that you are always leaving it to them. If you want to say, 'It's too cold to go out without an overcoat', you say, 'You may think it's too cold to go out without an overcoat', or 'Do you feel that it would be comfortable to go out without an overcoat in weather as cold as this?', or 'If you feel that no overcoat in this weather would be sensible, then all right, but I'd suggest that you'd be more comfortable with one'. You can also say, 'What I suggest to you, is that it would be downright foolish to go out without an overcoat'. Or 'I'm putting it to you for your consideration that only a fool would go out without an overcoat in this kind of weather'. Or even 'It's entirely for you to decide, Members of the Jury, and I won't insult your common sense by making any suggestion one way or the other, but do you really think that anyone, anyone in his right mind, would even *think* about going out in weather like that without an overcoat?'

You have made your point, have you not, with utmost clarity? You have conveyed to them that going out without an overcoat would have been sheer folly. Yet you have expressed no opinion whatsoever. It has all been done by suggestion. Note the phrases 'You may think', 'You may well feel', 'Do you think?', 'Can you believe that . . . ?', 'I suggest that . . .', 'I put it to you that . . .', and so on.

It follows from this that the words 'I think' have to be used with utmost caution. Used they certainly can be and very useful they are. 'I think it appears on page 32 of Your Lordship's bundle', 'I think you were on late duty that night, officer?', 'I think it will assist you, Members of the Jury, if I outline the facts very briefly and then go into a bit more detail once you've got the general picture'. But notice that in these examples the words 'I think' *do not introduce any opinion that you may hold as to the value of the evidence.* If they do that then you are falling into fundamental error. 'I think' must be used very carefully and you might find it helpful to avoid it altogether at the outset.

Essential aims

Keep your objections to an absolute minimum.   There will be times when your opponent will ask a question which you feel is improper. If the witness answers it then inadmissible evidence may be put before the jury. If such a question is asked you have to think like lightning because you have to decide whether to object and try to keep that answer from being given or whether to let it ride and thus to let the evidence in. Consider for a moment. Go back to the 'honest guide' rule and remember that you want, if at all possible, to be seen by the jury as playing all your cards face up. If you are constantly getting to your feet and objecting to questions that your opponent is asking you are running a terrible risk that you will lose the jury. What, they will ask themselves, is this lawyer trying to keep us from hearing? They will feel that there is more to this than meets the eye and you will find that they begin to suspect you rather than trust you.

On the other hand there are some bits of evidence which really ought not to be given and you simply have to make your objection. Work, therefore, on this basis: be willing to let in all inadmissible evidence that your opponent's questions call for unless such evidence is actually harmful to your client's case. If your opponent's question calls for an answer that offends against the rule against hearsay, then ask yourself quickly, does it matter if this evidence goes in? If it does not matter, then let it go. Don't object. If your opponent's question calls for an opinion, or if it is wildly hypothetical, or if it is composite, or if it is offensive in all manner of ways, always ask yourself 'Does it matter?' If it doesn't, let him get away with it. Regard it as a last resort to get up and object.

If you do object, then do it regretfully. Get to your feet and say something like, 'My Lord, I'm so sorry, but I wonder if that's a proper question by my friend'. Often, that is enough. The judge is quite likely to say to your opponent, 'That's bound to be right, isn't it, Mr Snooks?' which is a clear indication to your opponent that the judge is against him. That is usually the end of it. Sometimes it is you whom the judge is against. The question seems all right to him. You'll be met with the rejoinder 'Why?' or 'Why isn't it a proper question?' You deal with this by saying — still regretfully — 'Well, my friend seems to be asking the witness to tell us what somebody else said to him, My Lord, and that wouldn't be proper. But I'm entirely in Your Lordship's hands.'

By adopting this kind of approach you appear to the jury to be what you in fact are: somebody who is positively checking on whether the game is being played according to the rules. You are not an objector so much as a questioner. And you have raised the matter without hostility and in such a way as to make it clear that you will be perfectly happy with whatever the judge decides. If he is against you, you say contentedly, 'Very well, My Lord', and you sit down peacefully.

If the matter goes further than that and if the judge wants to discuss the propriety of the question with you and your opponent, then it is well nigh essential that the jury leave court while those discussions take place. It is almost inevitable that the judge will send them out without any application from you. If he does not, then you can say: 'I don't know, My Lord, perhaps the jury would like to stretch their legs for a little? This is a question of law that they don't have to be troubled with.' Then you are free to discuss the whole problem. You have lost no trust in the eyes of the jury whether successful or unsuccessful in your objection.

But the fundamental rule is clear. Do not object unless you simply have to.

Be as brief as you reasonably can be. This is very important indeed, but it does not mean that you must always be brief. There are undoubtedly occasions when it is essential to take your time and build slowly. Those, however, are rare. As a general rule brevity pays considerable dividends. The swifter you are the more likely you are to keep the attention of your audience and the less likely you are to bore them. If you keep your questions to a minimum you are likely to give the impression that you know exactly what you are doing, which enhances the jury's trust in you. If you are brief you are likely to appear businesslike and efficient which in turn earns the respect of both judge and jury. Above all, it earns their gratitude. Sitting there and listening is marvellous if the show is a good one, but in the nature of things a lot of what happens in court can be difficult, demands concentration and can be tiring. If you make every word count, if you avoid needless repetitions, if you avoid unnecessary hold-ups, if, indeed, you think of the court's time as ticking away like some expensive taximeter that *you* will have to pay for, then you will develop the right approach. Economise on time. Get fun out of doing it with as much elegant brevity as you can. Take the analogy of the oriental painter who uses the absolute minimum of brush strokes to achieve his effect, or of the surgeon whose incisions are as few as possible yet meticulously placed. The same ideals apply to advocacy. At the beginning of this book I emphasised that advocacy is a trade, a craft and an art. Remember this. Remember that the craftsman and the artist direct their efforts to where those efforts count, so that in the end it appears that there was no effort involved at all. Like judo, so with advocacy: movement, effort, activity — all should be kept to a minimum and applied only where they will produce the desired effect.

So work at it. Pare it down. Make almost a fetish out of it. If you do you will certainly gain a head start over the vast majority of advocates who behave as if they had all the time in the world. When you are opening the prosecution case to the jury do it as shortly as you possibly can. As Lord Lane CJ once observed, there are very few Crown Court cases that could not, at a pinch, be perfectly well opened in five minutes flat. Yet the average prosecutor takes half an hour or more. He tells the jury, sometimes word for word, what the witnesses are going to say. He puts plans and documents in front of them and tries to explain what they mean. None of it is really necessary. It is quite enough to sketch the position, tell them what the case is about and, with the judge's leave, call the first witness. The plans and the documents will be reached sooner or later and if the witnesses can't explain them then there is something amiss with the prosecution case.

Nor is it only a question of being brief and to the point in court itself. If you get into the brevity habit you will find that you economise on the number of witnesses that you call. You will also find yourself looking all the time to see how you can cut the proceedings down. You will probably find that this habit of thinking helps you to see what is truly relevant and what is not. There is always a pivotal point in a case. Get into the habit of searching for that point. Look for what it is that your case turns on. If you can strip a case down to its bare essentials then you will probably find that you can avoid the need for all manner of witnesses. You will probably find that there are a lot of things which you can quite happily admit.

Take, for instance, the common or garden case of burglary. The prosecution have to prove that the goods were stolen, so they have the loser as a witness. Your client's case is that it wasn't him. He cannot, on his case, dispute that the goods did in fact disappear from the loser's house. Very well. Admit it. If your opponent is going on at length in opening to the jury, telling them how he is going to prove that the loser's premises were broken into and his goods stolen, break in on him. Stand up and say swiftly, 'My friend will forgive me, My Lord, but I'm sure it will save everybody's time. It's the defendant's case that he wasn't the one who stole these goods. Since he wasn't there he can't deny what happened. I can therefore admit that the goods were stolen and my friend needn't take up any time in proving it.'

Make as many admissions as you can. Don't develop the habit of breaking into your opponent's speeches, but rather get up before he starts to call his witnesses and tell the judge and jury all those things that you are not going to dispute. Not only does it save time; it helps you in your standing as 'honest guide' and it contributes greatly to bringing everybody's minds to the real issues in the case. As an exercise in gamesmanship too it has its uses. If your opponent, all ready to prove his case, suddenly finds that nine tenths of his task has unexpectedly been done for him he might be caught just a little off balance for a moment. And nonplussing your opponent a little, it must be admitted, is certainly part of the fun of advocacy, providing it is done honestly and in good spirit.

Selecting the jury. In England and Wales our opportunities for choosing the jurors are almost non-existent. In the United States it is one of the important tasks of the advocate to find out as much as he possibly can about the people who are in the 'jury pool'. In cases where a great deal is at stake American advocates have been known to take to court with them trained psychologists who will observe the jurors as they come into the jury box, will listen to the questions that are put to them before they are selected on to the jury and will advise the advocate as to any bias that a juror may be likely to have. Before a trial begins in the United States the advocate will know a great deal about his jury. He will know what they have to say about certain prejudices: he will know whether they are rich, poor, educated, uneducated, widowed, married, childless or parents, where they live and what they do for a living. He will, in most American courts, have been able to talk directly to them, asking them questions and receiving their answers on a one-to-one basis, and he will have been able to 'dismiss' many a juror whom he thought would not be helpful to his cause.

In Britain we have none of this. We may know the name of the juror, and that is it. Until some years ago we had the right to know their addresses and occupations as well, but then, with one fell, executive, discretionary stroke of a pen in the Lord Chancellor's Department, those rights to know were taken away from us. About the same time our right to challenge jurors was curtailed. It used to be the right of every defendant to challenge off seven jurors without giving any reason for so doing. That was reduced from seven to three, then abolished altogether. These curtailments of our right of challenge took place, so it is said, late at night in Parliament with no debate, no objection and no vote. The civil servants wanted it and the opinion of the legal profession was, apparently, not consulted. Well, that's the way things sometimes happen in England.

We still have the right to challenge jurors off 'for cause'. If you discover that a particular juror has a personal relationship with one of the parties, or has personal knowledge of some aspect of the case, that juror can be challenged 'for cause.' But how are you to know if you have 'cause' unless you are allowed to ask questions of the jurors in advance of their being empanelled? Unless you find your mother-in-law coming into the jury box, or unless your client points out that a juror is known to him, challenge for cause is a virtually meaningless right. These diminutions in our rights are consistent with the way successive British governments have vandalised trial by jury.

Do remember, however, that your client probably knows none of this, and may very well be thoroughly confused when he hears the clerk of the court intone at him that he has the right to object to jurors. Tell him in advance that these rights are vestigial and will almost certainly not apply to his case, but that if he recognises any juror he is to let you know forthwith. Advocates so often forget to explain this, and it is distressing for the client, as well as undignified, to have one's assistant running to the back of the court and whispering tardy advice while the jury is being empanelled.

Six

Speeches for the prosecution

When prosecuting, remember Lord Lane's advice and *keep it as short as you can*. Always explain to the jury at some stage before you begin to call your evidence that it is the prosecution who bring the case and that it is for the prosecution to prove the case. Explain that it is your job to convince them that there is no sensible alternative to a guilty verdict and tell them that if you don't convince them of that, on the evidence, then they will have to acquit. If you are straight with them, if you tell them honestly that this is the job you are taking on before them, you will have started to get their sympathy. Too often the advocate who is prosecuting just confines himself to the time-worn phrase, 'If you are not satisfied on this evidence then it will be your pleasure to acquit'. He thereby misses a marvellous chance of reaching out to the jury. If someone says, in effect, 'I'll tell you what I'm going to try to do. I'll tell you how I'm going to try to do it. You watch and tell me at the end how I've done', then the jury cannot help but feel a little sympathetic towards him. He has made himself a little human, a little vulnerable, certainly a little humble. He has also started to establish himself as an 'honest guide'.

So don't throw away your advantage of having the first chance to talk to the jury. In 1982 a fascinating book appeared on the working of the House of Lords as the highest appeal court of the United Kingdom (*Law Lords*, Macmillan). The author, Alan Paterson, dwells on the terrific advantage which is given to the advocate who has the privilege of 'opening the facts' to his tribunal; and he quotes an endearing observation by the daughter of Lord Atkin. 'When my father used to tell us about the facts of his cases', she recalls, 'it was impossible to imagine what the other side could possibly hope to achieve. It seemed that there could only be one possible outcome of the case.' I am paraphrasing, but the message is so very clear: in the hands of a real advocate the chance to have the *first* word to his tribunal is an enormous advantage. So do please remember that. Do not appear to be some kind of machine, some kind of functionary. There they are, a totally captive audience. All yours. Take their interest. Cultivate their sympathy. Set yourself up truthfully as an 'honest guide'. Above all talk to them and not at them.

One of the best beginnings I ever heard by a prosecutor came in a drugs case. The clerk of the court had just finished reading over the charge that went something like this:

> Members of the Jury. William Sykes is charged on one count on this indictment in that he on the — day of — 19— at London Airport, Heathrow, was knowingly concerned in the fraudulent evasion of the prohibition on the importation of a class A drug namely diamorphine hydrochloride contrary to, etc. . . .

Prosecuting counsel got to his feet.

> 'May it please you, My Lord', he said, and then paused and looked at the jury. Then he grinned at them.
> 'I'll bet', he said, 'you didn't understand a word of that!'

And they looked at him with delight. Of course they hadn't understood it.

> 'Knowingly concerned in the fraudulent evasion of the prohibition on the importation of . . . etc., etc.'

He paused again, as they a watched him intently, waiting to see what this first, real human being was going to say next.

> 'Don't worry, ladies and gentlemen', he said. 'That mouthful of lawyer's gobbledegook actually means something. And I'll tell you what it is.'

They were twelve people absolutely attentive to this nice, sensible chap.

> 'What it means, Members of the Jury', he said, 'is that this defendant, William Sykes, is accused of old-fashioned smuggling.'

Another pause.

'What the prosecution accuse this defendant of is smuggling into this country a drug that most people know by the name of heroin.'

And another slight pause as the smiles fade and the nastiness of the drug gets across to the jury.

'What you have to do, Members of the Jury, is listen to the evidence and then tell us if this defendant was indeed involved in smuggling heroin into this country as the prosecution say he was.'

He then told them that customs officers had opened a parcel at the post office addressed to the defendant, that there had been heroin in it, that they had replaced the heroin with a harmless substance, that the parcel had been re-sealed and delivered and that immediately after delivery there had been a raid by customs investigators. The defendant had made admissions of his guilt in writing as well as in conversation with the investigators and they would hear about this in due course. Listen to the evidence, he said. If they felt that there was any doubt that Mr Sykes was knowingly involved with the heroin then they had to acquit him. If, on the other hand, they were left feeling sure that he *was* knowingly involved, then the verdict would be guilty. It was as simple as that. Now let's listen to the evidence.

It took about three minutes in all. With complete justification the jury loved it. He had been totally honest, totally fair, totally open. He had been brief and he had seemed what he was: a decent individual doing his job with decency and understanding.

Always remember that people are people. Every individual has some totally unexpected talent or strength no matter how coarse or simple-minded the external appearance may be. In that composite jury-animal there will be all manner of strengths and weaknesses. But they are people. And all people respond to being talked to with openness and frankness. We call them 'speeches', but as has been said already and will be said again, you should never make a speech as such to a jury. Talk to them. Tell them what you want to tell them. Do this and they will listen to you. Apart from anything else, it's so much easier than making a speech.

When prosecuting, remember what you are trying to do. You are trying to place before the jury a certain amount of evidence and then trying to make them see that the only reasonable inference to be drawn from that evidence is that the defendant is guilty. If the time comes when the defendant goes into the witness box then you will want, by cross-examining him, to show that he ought not to be relied on in what he says. The same is true of the witnesses called for the defence. In the end, it isn't more complicated than that. It can be done very simply and very briefly. And it is to be noticed that the prosecutors who do it this way are very successful in their task.

I was defending a man once who told a very improbable story indeed. Had I been asked to say whether I thought he was guilty, I would have had to say in all honesty that I couldn't believe him. Yet when he went into the witness box and stuttered through his evidence, prosecuting counsel cross-examined him for a total of 17½ hours! Some questions he repeated fifteen times. He went around and around, repeating himself woefully and constantly accusing the defendant of lying. An hour was all that he really needed. The jury got restive then bored and then indignant. They got so downright sorry for the defendant, being pushed around day after day by this blunt instrument in a wig, that when the time came they acquitted him. It was probably a miscarriage of justice, and if it was then it was certainly contributed to, if not entirely caused, by a boring and bullying prosecutor.

When you come to your final speech the first thing to ask yourself is 'should I make a speech at all?' Familiarise yourself with the Court of Appeal cases which discuss the propriety of making a closing speech for the prosecution. If you decide that you are going to make a final speech, remember what your task is. Remember that the jury have heard the evidence. Don't do what so many prosecutors do, tonelessly going through what every witness said. Remind them of what you were trying to do, summarise the points for and against you as briefly as you can, emphasise what you think needs emphasising and then *ask* them whether the prosecution has convinced them. Then sit down. Aim to do it in 10 minutes flat. The shorter your observations, the punchier they will inevitably be. The shorter they are, the more likely they are to be remembered. The shorter you are, the more confident you are likely to appear. Give them a few phrases to hold on to. If a conviction is the right verdict then you ought to be able to set out on one side of a piece of foolscap why it's the right verdict. Don't go boringly on. Be as brief as you possibly can, consistent with saying what you have to.

Remember that you are not (or certainly ought not to be) trying to get a conviction. You are there to make sure that the testimony comes before the jury properly, fairly and in accordance with the rules of evidence. You are there to assist the jury in drawing the proper inferences from that evidence. The more you remember this and the less you strive to get the defendant convicted the more successful you are likely to be.

Above all, whenever you are prosecuting, be as nice as you can be. Niceness is one of the most powerful weapons in the prosecutor's armoury. Also, it goes without saying, make sure you come across as scrupulously fair. The prosecutor who is unquestionably nice and obviously fair is, far more often than not, lethally effective.

Seven

Speeches for the defence

The high points of advocacy?

The defence speeches in a jury trial are, or ought to be, the high points of advocacy. No opportunity in modern life brings you so close to the platform of classical oratory. The political hustings hardly compare, and except for a once-in-45-years national crisis, Parliament doesn't provide the opportunity either. When coming to make the closing speech, particularly, you are the twentieth century descendant of the great orators of history. Think about that and think about it with awe. You may become aware of the responsibility that you have blithely taken on your shoulders. You are carrying on the great tradition of a past that included Demosthenes, Cicero, Erskine, Birkett and Choate. And the way in which you and your contemporaries carry on that tradition will decide what remains of that tradition when you have come to the end of your career.

Although history seems to be studied less and less these days, with the result that a lot of you may be, as it were, stranded in the present, nevertheless that history is there. Go and look for it. If you have never read any Demosthenes, find some. Even more, find and read some Cicero. One of his techniques is alive and well and living in the courts today. We'll come to it later. Do, please, indulge in the sheer pleasure of reading Erskine wherever you can find him, and study as much as you can of Birkett. The memoirs of Birkett's clerk, A. E. Bowker, called *Behind the Bar* will start you off very well. Read Marjoribank's biography of Marshall Hall.

If you read around like this one thing ought to strike you above all else. It is that times change, and with those changing times, so fashions change as well. The language of Demosthenes had more in common with the language of the Victorian lawyer than with our modern language of advocacy. Today our language is much, much crisper. Our sentences are much shorter. The words we use are much less Latinised. Our references and allusions are much less classical and biblical. This is because our education and that of our audience has changed. Juries are no longer chosen only from the heads of Edwardian households whose property was above a certain value. Now they come from all stations in life. Sixty years ago you could reasonably expect your juror to know that 'omnia Gallia' was 'in tres partes divisa' and that a shibboleth was a subtle badge of identity. The old juryman expected convoluted sentences structured with care and decoration. Look at the Royal Courts of Justice in the Strand, or even more so the Victoria Law Courts in Birmingham. Their architecture well reflects the advocates' language of their time. Then look at the modern extension of the Old Bailey and really take in the difference. Language and its use change enormously in a hundred years. Never forget that your jury is a modern jury, their thinking and feeling the product of the cinema, the tele-vision, the welfare state, tabloid newspapers, fast food, pre-digested news items, electrical and electronic everything. Their thinking and feeling is probably more *visual* than it has ever been in the history of mankind. They are not used to words as their primary source of information and of understanding, but to visual images and swiftly edited visual images at that.

Remember this and *then* read the greats of the past. You will see all the rules suggested in this book being put into effect and a lot more besides. Realise how well adjusted to *their* audience the great advo-cates were. Read them and learn how they adhered to the basic rules.

But applying our first rule of knowing your audience and adjusting to it, you will realise that today's final speech will not sound like oratory. It will sound much more like a reasoned talk on the radio, much nearer to Alistair Cooke's 'Letter from America' than to Mark Antony's 'I come to bury Caesar, not to praise him'. Bear that in mind. It is downright dangerous, today, to swing into anything approaching a purple passage. Beware the broad gesture, the extravagant phrase, and, again, think very carefully before daring to raise your voice.

But having said all that, the defence speech calls for all that it ever did and all the skills that you have developed as an advocate are needed here. In your defence speeches you must have *all* the rules in mind, and if you are doing your duty properly you will get across to the jury the enormity of their task. You will make them feel the shocking responsibility of sitting in judgment on another citizen. You will make them deeply and wholly aware of the need for them to be *sure* before they return a verdict of guilty. You will make them realise what an ugly failure of the whole process would be involved if they convicted an innocent person. You will show them why they should not convict. You will help them to see how they can feel that they are doing the right thing when they pronounce your client not guilty.

You can, therefore, divide your defence speech into three parts. I do not mean by this that you split it up into three watertight compartments. You may be able to mingle them with great success. What is meant is that there should be three objectives:

(a) To make the jury realise what their duty actually is.
(b) To face the difficulties in the evidence against you and to suggest how those difficulties do *not* mean that the verdict must be one of guilty.
(c) To show the jury how they may rightly and sensibly acquit.

If you intend to call the accused himself together with only character witnesses, then the defence have no right to any opening speech. If, on the other hand, the defence intend to call any witness as to fact, then the defending advocate is entitled to address the jury before calling his evidence as well as at the end of the trial. Two speeches instead of one, in fact. There used to be a rule which restricted the opening speech to a mere outlining of the evidence that the defence intended to call. But that is no longer the case. The Court of Appeal some years ago said that in his opening speech defending counsel ought not to be confined thus. So he may now say to the jury whatever seems proper at this half-way stage in the trial.

In the view of some advocates this is a great opportunity never to be wasted. Others take the view that the dangers inherent in the opening speech make it wiser to avoid it altogether. It is something for you to decide for yourself, but let us look at the pros and cons. They need to be considered somewhat carefully, and the dangers arise mainly out of the nature of that other strange animal known as 'the witness'. I haven't said much about witnesses so far and the time has probably come to interpolate a few observations on the genus.

Witnesses

They come in all shapes and sizes and of all ages, just about. The judges do not like seeing young children and very old people brought to court to give evidence, but between the ages of about ten and eighty a person may well find him or herself being called. They can be classified in all manner of ways but for your purposes you need go no further at the moment than to be aware of the major species. One division of witnesses is into what might be called 'professional' and 'non-professional'. Into the professional category go all policemen, police-surgeons, scientific officers from the forensic laboratories, inquiry agents, process servers and certain experts. Such experts include those consulting engineers, surveyors, architects, physicians, psychiatrists and surgeons who habitually make themselves available to advise lawyers and who therefore get called with some frequency to give evidence in court. Into the non-professional category goes everybody else, everybody, in fact, whose occupation or life-style makes it extremely unlikely, save by some unexpected event, that they will ever be called as a witness in court.

The obvious difference between the two groupings is that the professional witness is likely to be familiar with the court-room and its methods while the non-professional is likely to find the whole experience of giving evidence an overwhelmingly unfamiliar one. Cast your mind back to the last occasion when you did something for the very first time, and recall how unfamiliar it felt. Indeed, play the game of going back in your memory to search for something which was as totally unfamiliar to you as giving evidence must be to the average citizen. It is completely new. The court-room is something that the average person has seen only on television. The antique uniforms, whether they look imposing or funny, take the occasion quite out of the ordinary for your man on the Clapham omnibus. Were this not all unfamiliar enough for your witness, he is now asked to do something which most people are irrationally afraid of doing: he is asked to make his solitary voice heard in public, to speak, alone, in a crowd of listening people. For many, the thought of having to do such a thing brings them out in a mild sweat, just as the thought of potholing or mountain climbing frightens a lot of others. To the average non-professional witness the experience of testifying may well be a little dream-like in its strangeness. Remember that. Remember it for this reason: you would never choose to turn for help to someone who was in a dream-like state of disorientation. Rather you would expect him to turn to you. If you were foolish enough to expect help from a person in that condition and let the outcome of your case hang on getting that help, then you would deserve to lose. *This is a quite fundamental rule in dealing with the non-professional witness: never look to him for help.* If you were seeking to rescue someone from a cliff face you would hope for nothing more from him than that he kept still while you got the rope around him and then put his hands and feet in the places that you indicated. The rest is up to you. Never expect help from your non-professional witness.

Oddly, enough, the rule applies equally to the professional witness. The expert may sound incredibly in command of the situation in his report and in his 'proof' of evidence (i.e. the written statement which sets out what he is expected to say). When you meet him in conference he may again seem as clear and as firm in his view as you could possibly wish. Put him in the witness box and watch him change. It is unbelievable to realise, as you will, how many professional witnesses, experts familiar with their subject and with court proceedings, just come apart like wet cardboard toys when actually giving evidence. The expert engineer who explained it so forcefully to you in conference suddenly changes his story, hedges his bets, piles on the ifs and buts and becomes willing to agree to anything. Policemen under cross-examination, asked about things they are not expecting to be asked about, can dissolve into embarrassed 'don't knows' and admissions that they failed to follow the rules. Doctors, accountants, surveyors, experts of all kinds, are all subject to the same curious rule. When advocates find an expert witness who really is clear and firm, they comment to each other afterwards. The exception is noticeable.

So, with all due respect to expert witnesses everywhere, and with apologies to that proportion of them who really are good, the advice to you must be the same: *never look to a witness for help.* We will come in a later chapter to the question of how to examine and cross-examine witnesses, but this much may be said now: assume that your witness is, as likely as not, going to let you down in some way or other. Before

ever that witness goes into the witness box you should have thought about where that let-down might come and you should have given attention to what you are going to do about it. You should certainly have a clear plan about exactly how you are going to question the witness, how far you intend to go, exactly what you hope the witness is going to say and exactly where you think you are going to be able to help him. *You* are the leader of the mountain rescue team: *he* is the frightened casualty on the cliff face. Of course this is an exaggerated way of putting it and of course there are exceptions. But get the principle of this rule firmly under your belt and you will be likely to adopt the right approach.

The other major division of witnesses is into 'friendly' and 'unfriendly'. This is another obvious distinction but the same rule applies here, too. You will no doubt get help from a friendly witness, but approach that witness in the expectation that, willing though he may be, he is likely to let you down. Again it is *you* who must plan how most safely to draw his evidence out of him: it is you who are, and ought to be, in command.

The opening speech

Having said this much, let us get back to the opening speech to the jury. Its inherent dangers, or some of them, ought now to be obvious, and two out of the three principal dangers can be stated thus: by opening your case for the defence to the jury and by telling them what evidence you intend to call: (a) you run the risk of finding that your witnesses fail to come up to proof, fail to testify as you promised the jury they would and thereby make horribly public the difference between what you expected them to say and what they did say; and (b) you run the different and subtler risk that your witnesses indeed say what you promised they would, but say it in a way very different from the way in which you said it. Coming from you it sounded fine: coming from them it somehow fell flat.

These are two very real dangers, and all of us who have opened incautiously to a jury have found ourselves wallowing in the muddy traps that they create for the unwary. The third danger in the opening defence speech is that by disclosing in advance what your evidence is (you hope) going to be, you give your opponent time to think about it, time to set fresh inquiries afoot perhaps, time even in which to produce rebutting evidence, but certainly time in which to consider how he might cross-examine these witnesses, the nature of whose evidence you are now helpfully laying before him.

Thus the dangers. And you can see how real they can be.

The advantages of the opening speech, on the other hand, are equally great, and if the existence of the dangers is clearly borne in mind and if your speech is designed to avoid them, far more advantage than risk can be brought out of an opening. Think what you can do with it. Realise that you may, if you want to, divide your closing speech into two parts, and effectively have one at the beginning of your evidence and one at the end. And having realised that the whole of what you want to say to the jury can be spread between your opening and closing speech, just think of the advantages that that presents to you. You are now free for the first time to lead the jury's thinking where *you* want it to go. They ought to know you by now, and they ought to trust you, ought to have seen where you were going, ought to have as clear a picture of what your case is as it was possible for you to give them as you made admissions and cross-examined.

But now you may claim their undivided attention and have the chance to talk to them direct and, subject to the rules of laying the ground for comment and of not giving evidence or opinion yourself, the chance to say to them what you will. If you feel so inclined you can talk to them now, rather than at the end of the case, about the burden of proof. You may, if you wish, comment at this stage about the inadequacies of your opponent's case. You can comment on what has happened in the trial so far. Anything that is more usually said in your closing speech you are permitted to say now, if you think that helps you.

Particularly, you can and you ought to prepare the minds of the jury for the evidence that they are about to hear. Do not tell them in detail what witness X or witness Y is going to say. Apart from anything else you must be very careful to avoid giving evidence. 'Mr X will say...' is frowned on as being against the 'no evidence from the advocate' rule. Instead, tell them in the briefest *outline* what they are likely to hear. Do not say, for instance: 'I shall be calling Mr Smith, who, I anticipate, will tell you that he was the owner of the goods and that he obtained them from X and passed them in the normal course of trading to the defendant'. Say instead: 'I shall be calling Mr Smith who I hope will be able to help you as to the ownership of the goods that we've been hearing evidence about'. Doing it this way, you do not run the risk that your witness will let you down. You have not told the jury what he is going to say, so you will not later appear to have egg on your face when he says something else. You also avoid the risk of being thought to be giving evidence, and you have the further advantage of rousing the jury's curiosity. You have promised them what you hope will turn out to be a bit of help. You haven't told them exactly what it is. They will be waiting for it with interest. In this way you avoid all the dangers outlined earlier.

Preparing the minds of the jury for what they are about to hear, it cannot be over-emphasised, does not mean telling the jury *the detail* of the evidence you are about to call. It means something quite different. You are about to call your client. Your client is perhaps someone who has never given evidence before. Prepare them for that. Your client is probably going to be cut about in cross-examination. Prepare them for that. You fear that your client may seem in the box to be a shifty, oily, unattractive illiterate. Prepare them for that. Your witnesses may be of bad character, of uncertain memory or even of shakingly nervous disposition. Prepare them for all these things.

Prepare them even for the irritation that you are all going to suffer because your witness has a voice which it is difficult to hear. Nothing is so stupidly annoying. The police all have voices that are trained to be heard. All advocates are nicely audible or ought to be. Only some judges and witnesses don't speak up, and only witnesses get shouted at for it. The fear of giving evidence is likely to dry up a nervous person's voice anyway and often does, and this witness's discomfort is mightily aggravated by having the judge testily repeating 'Oh! Do speak up!' In such circumstances the witness can and often does start to come across to the jury as boring and maybe even a bit simple-minded, and since you are seeking to rely on his evidence, holding it out as strong and trustworthy, this is the last thing you want. But if you deal with it in advance, if you tell the jury that these are ordinary people that they are about to hear, people unfamiliar with the court-room who will probably be confused by the surroundings anyway (and even more confused when nagged to speak up) — if you grasp this little nettle in advance, all the sting will be gone when it happens. Prepare them for it.

Make absolutely sure that you tell them in advance about cross-examination. Tell them that by giving evidence the defendant is doing something inherently courageous: he is presenting himself to the prosecutor to be cross-examined, to be asked as many questions over as many hours or as many days as the prosecutor pleases. Make them realise what this means. Prepare them for the potentially pitiful sight that they may well witness, the pathetically ill-matched contest in words between petty ex-criminal and trained and experienced advocate. Without so much as the hint of a purple passage, get this message across. As in everything else discussed so far this, too, is an honest task. It *is* an unequal contest when accused and prosecutor meet face to face, and in your opening speech you have the totally honest opportunity of making this clear to the jury.

You can also say this. You can tell the jury that if a witness is lying, then cross-examination is regarded as the best tool available to show that he is lying. And you can tell them that if your client is lying then they will no doubt see this exposed to them by your opponent's cross-examination. When, as is sometimes the case, your client comes through unscathed, then you may with justification point to this fact in your final speech. Apart from anything else, telling the jury in advance of the terrors of cross-examination puts a heavy burden on your opponent to deliver the goods. And as has been said before, legitimately wrong-footing your opponent is part of the art and craft of the job. It is, after all, a kind of miniaturised warfare, is the trial, conducted with all manner of rules of decency and honesty; but a kind of warfare it is.

Another thing you may want to do at this stage is to explain to them what their attitude ought to be towards the evidence that they are about to hear. If you consider the criminal burden of proof for a moment, you will realise that a conviction cannot be proper if the jury feel that the accused and his witnesses *might* have been telling the truth. If the jury think that the accused *may* have been telling them the truth, then they must acquit. The prosecution evidence on the other hand has to convince them to the point when they are *sure*. All this implies, or should imply, a change of gear when the jury come to listen to defence evidence. They are not listening with a view to being convinced now. They are listening with a view to 'wondering whether'. If they are left feeling, 'I wonder', then they ought to acquit.

Explain this to them. Use analogies or metaphor (even hyperbole if you must). Try it in the simplest language preferably, but in your opening speech do get across to the jury that they have now got to make a change of gear. The accused is on his own. The Crown, with all the power of the State behind it, chose to arrest and charge and indict him and make him sit in this dock in this court with people from the prison service beside him. The finger of accusation has been pointing at him throughout the trial and all he has had to help him is you as his advocate and the *presumption that he is innocent.*

The jury must be made to realise what that presumption means. That presumption is that it is a mistake for your client to be sitting in the dock at all. That presumption is that they've got the wrong man. That man in the dock is innocent. Innocent as the judge is innocent, as the jury are innocent, as the ushers are innocent. That is what the presumption means. The jury are trying an innocent man. Until the evidence has overwhelmed that presumption so that it is gone, flattened, broken up, the jury must keep thinking of the defendant as innocent.

They didn't when the trial began. Their natural, human instinct when they first saw the defendant was to wonder 'What's he done?' They start off by assuming that the defendant is guilty. Otherwise, they feel, why would he be in a court of law, sitting in the dock? It is natural to feel this way. It's not only jurors. At a court martial I was doing years ago a squadron leader who was to sit on my court the following day was buying me a drink and telling me how reliable court-martial justice was. In all slightly tipsy seriousness he said: 'Wheel the guilty bastard in! We'll give him a fair trial and decide what to do with him.'

I protested.

'Come off it,' he said. 'They've got to be guilty or it wouldn't have got this far.' He explained the summary taking process to me. I could see his point. Thankfully he could see mine. 'Don't worry,' he told me. 'If the evidence doesn't stack up we'll let him off. It's got to be a fair trial.' I can't remember if they did let him off but it brought home to me early in my career what the defending advocate is up against.

Your court, your jury, your magistrates, are all human. They almost all start with that gut feeling that the fellow must be guilty. It's a feeling that in turn comes out of another gut feeling — the presumption that things are being done properly, that there hasn't been a mistake made, that things are functioning normally. If we didn't work in accordance with that natural presumption, then we would hesitate to light a gas stove, to turn on an electrical switch, to drive a car on the roads. We would go about in a perpetual state of suppressed agitation, waiting for something to go wrong. But we don't. We assume that everything is all right. We have to. And our trust is repeatedly rewarded. Our gut-presumption that things are more or less as they should be is vindicated time and time again, almost a hundred per cent of the time in fact.

This is what you have to work against. This is what you have to displace, and replace with the presumption that everything is *anything but all right*. That's the wrong man they've got there. That is what the presumption of innocence is all about: that is what we mean by the burden of proof. And it is the opposite of that strong, inbred presumption that everything is as it should be. That is what *you* must make the jury understand. They'll change gear willingly enough if you get that across to them. They will be prepared to listen in a completely different way once you have made them see and feel in a completely different way.

But remember: this is down to you. The prosecution will have dealt with it in hardly more than a perfunctory sentence or two, delivered almost as an afterthought sometimes, and the judge will have said nothing as yet. This is not only your task, but this is the first chance you will have had to get this point across to the jury. You may feel it is an opportunity not to be missed.

If you do decide to make an opening speech then indicate this to the judge by the following sentence: 'My Lord, I shall be calling other evidence'. Then turn to the jury and get on with it. By that indication to the judge you remind him that you are perfectly aware of the restriction which prevents you from opening unless you are calling other evidence as to fact apart from that of the defendant. It is, furthermore, a convention to say this before starting an opening speech, and, you may notice, an exception to the rule about asking the judge's permission for just about everything.

The closing speech

That said about the opening, let us come to the closing speech, and go back to the objectives that we noted earlier. What has been said as to the burden of proof and the presumption of innocence applies all the way through both speeches. Deal with them in both if you feel that you can do this without losing your audience. Make a rondo out of it if you feel you are keeping their interest and sympathy. Do it any way you like but get that message across. As for the other things that your closing speech should achieve, let us restate them and at the same time add one more objective, thus making four in all. They are as follows:

(a) Make the jury realise what their duty actually is.
(b) Face your difficulties and show how they do not necessarily mean that your client should be found guilty.
(c) Show the jury how they may rightly acquit, i.e. 'show them the way home'.
(d) Use the 'anti-boot' device, if necessary.

Let us deal with these in turn, coming to the last of them in the next chapter.

Make the jury understand their duty   I have largely dealt with this in considering the presumption of innocence and the burden of proof. As has been already emphasised it is your task to make them realise the importance of what they are doing in sitting in judgment on a fellow citizen, and the deep responsibility of understanding and applying the presumption of innocence. It really does bear repetition that this is *your* task. Nobody else will deal with it properly. Some judges pass over the matter as if reciting some kind of litany, dealing in as few words as possible with this principal corner-stone on which our criminal justice rests. Why they do it is difficult to understand. So don't leave it to anybody else. I shall make no suggestion as to what words or analogies to use. It is essentially a matter for you. As long as you understand this vital need, and always keep thinking about better ways of getting this fundamental point across to the jury, that is enough.

Face your difficulties   Unless you have been unlucky in the way the trial has gone, so that your position is quite hopeless, then by the time you come to your final speech there ought to be a really live issue to be decided by the jury. You ought to take the points made by the prosecution, the points which the prosecution say add up to your client's guilt, and examine them individually. Take them and hold them and, with the jury, consider their value. Don't be afraid. Nothing diminishes your opponent's best points so much in the eyes of the jury as the sight of you calmly picking them up one by one and in a completely relaxed manner giving them a most careful inspection.

If they are indeed good points against you, concede that they are. Say over and over again that they provide powerful evidence against you. Mark Antony told the Roman mob seven times that Brutus was an honourable man. By the fifth time Brutus had taken to his heels. Coming from you, a concession that a point is a strong one against you will tend to diminish its strength. Don't ask why — I cannot give you the answer, but I have seen it work on many occasions. It has probably got something to do with our innate respect for fearlessness. If you see someone calmly handling a venomous snake and calmly telling you that this is a venomous snake, you supply with your thinking the bit that has been left unspoken — 'but handled properly there is no need to worry about it'.

The mere act of facing your difficulties without fuss or anxiety tends to reduce them in the eyes of your audience. And if you keep contentedly asserting that it is a good point against you, the more willing the jury is likely to be to receive the explanation which they know you have waiting for them. 'A very venomous snake,' you say, 'very venomous indeed'. And they are all waiting willingly for your explanation like an audience waiting for the resolution of a chord of music. Your answer to the point may well be welcomed with a feeling of satisfaction.

Now, it is not being suggested that you will achieve this straightaway. It has to be done with quiet confidence, and as all experienced advocates well remember, that is a commodity that you don't have much of during your early days. But try to understand this point and aim to put it into operation. In the final speech you *must* face the case that has been made against you. So do it contentedly. Take each point, concede that it's a venomous snake and then give your answer to it. Very rarely is there no answer, otherwise the case would have started with a plea of guilty.

When you have picked up and looked comfortably at the whole of your opponent's points, push them aside. Come now to what the defence evidence is all about. Tell them that they know already everything that the defence relies upon and summarise it very briefly. You will have referred to a lot, if not all, of your defence evidence during your 'snake-handling', as you answered the prosecution's strong points one by one. So give them one brief summary of the whole thing. Which leads nicely on to the next objective.

'Show them the way home'   This is a well-known phrase among advocates, and it is one of the most important rules of advocacy. Let me explain it as best I can. For a jury to come back with a verdict of not guilty is sometimes very difficult for them. They *are* left wondering whether the defendant did it or not and so they intellectually realise that not guilty is the only proper verdict. The difficulty is that half a dozen decent-looking and decent-sounding police officers have given clear evidence of the defendant's guilt, and if the jury come back with a not guilty verdict they will be appearing to reject that police evidence in its entirety. They don't like the idea of doing that. It is not easy for them. The not guilty verdict, they feel, is the right one, but by delivering that correct verdict they feel uncomfortable, they feel as if they will be doing wrong at the same time as doing right. They are left with an emotional conflict. They feel so reluctant to brand the police as liars that they are stuck. One way in which they can get out of the cleft stick is to look again at their proposed verdict of not guilty. The question may well get re-opened, and once re-opened it could well be answered the opposite way and against the interests of your client.

If this is so with a jury, imagine how very much more difficult it is when you are appearing before a magistrate. Neither jury nor magistrate like the idea of finding that the police have been less than honest. They most certainly don't like declaring as much by their verdict. Their reluctance may be so great that they would prefer to sacrifice your client rather than come out with what they feel would be a verdict against the police. Accordingly it is very dangerous indeed for an advocate to leave such a stark choice before the tribunal. Sometimes it is indeed unavoidable, but such cases are rather rare.

The advocate should always aim to avoid landing jury or magistrate in such a dilemma, because it makes it *difficult* for them. If they might even feel inclined to acquit your client it is essential that you should have shown them how this could be done *easily*. You must 'show them the way home', show them how they can acquit in comfort, show them how a not guilty verdict will be felt to be sensible and proper by any right-minded person who has listened to the proceedings. You must show them how no adverse comment will necessarily be implied as to anybody's conduct if they acquit.

Now, after all that has been said in this book about honesty, this is where the advocate has to flirt with dishonesty. It is a pity but it is a fact of life. It will stick in your throat on many occasions. So try to understand it and realise the dishonesty in which you may have to get involved is that kind of dishonesty that lubricates the functioning of the world.

'How do you like my new hat, dear?'
'Simply delightful, darling.'

'How am I, doctor? Is it serious?'
'Not at all. Just take it easily now.'

'Sorry about the squalor. Do you think you'll be all right?'
'Not a bit of it, I'll be very comfortable here.'

They are all lies. But they are the kind of lies without which society simply fails to function. Most of the time they are passed off as illustrations of tact on the part of the liar.

Let us go by way of illustration to a trifling little case in a magistrates' court. The charge was that the defendant had been drunk and disorderly in the Marylebone Road late one night. What made the case different from thousands of others was that the client was a middle-aged gentleman of the utmost respectability. He was a retired major of a good regiment and the brother of a senior and rather distinguished solicitor. They were both liverymen and had that evening attended an informal livery gathering. The major had declined the offer of a lift home. It was a fine night and although it was well past midnight he felt like a stroll, intending to hail a taxi when he tired of walking. He had two interesting characteristics: he was an extremely peppery individual, very short on charm, and — like Field-Marshal Lord Montgomery — he was a confirmed non-drinker and non-smoker. He bade his solicitor brother goodnight and walked from the centre of the City until, at the Marylebone Road, he felt the need to urinate. He went behind some railings into a dark alcove and as he emerged again into what had seemed to be the deserted street he was approached by two very young policemen.

The major's account of what happened then was to the effect that the two youngsters accused him of loitering with intent. He told them rather charmlessly that he was doing nothing of the kind and they made him turn out his pockets, passing offensive remarks about his possessions, laughing and joking about him and constantly calling him 'Dad'. He was not accustomed to being treated thus and delivered himself of what lay upon his mind. The young policemen started poking him repeatedly in the chest, making fun of him and imputing all manner of indecent reasons to his being out at that time of night. When the major well and truly lost his temper and declared that he would report their conduct to their superiors they turned nasty, arrested him, called up a car, took him back to the police station and had him charged with being drunk and disorderly. His protests to the station sergeant were ignored and he was locked up for the night. Despite shrill demands for a call to be made to his brother and for a doctor to be brought, he was left to himself in his cell and the next morning taken before the court with all the other drunks where he demanded and got an adjournment.

His case eventually came on before a well-known convicting magistrate. The two young policemen testified that they had watched him come out from behind some railings and go staggering and shouting down the road, accosting a woman whom he encountered. When they approached him he became highly abusive and went to strike them with his rolled umbrella. His eyes were glazed and his breath smelled of drink. They arrested him. The station sergeant confirmed the drunken condition. No, he had made no request for a solicitor or doctor.

For the defence the Major gave his version. His total abstinence from drink was testified to by three acquaintances of rank and distinction including two with whom he had spent the evening before the arrest.

They and his solicitor brother were able to swear that he had had no alcohol that night and that he was in his normal condition. They all agreed that his temper had a somewhat short fuse and that he did not suffer fools gladly.

He *had* to be acquitted, but before that magistrate the defending advocate had to tread very, very delicately. He could so easily have proclaimed what overwhelmingly appeared to be the truth of the situation, namely that a couple of young thugs in police uniform had disgraced the trust placed in them and with youthful malice had picked on an elderly gentleman and baited him until he threatened to report them. Then they had protected themselves by a course of conduct that involved false imprisonment, malicious prosecution and perjury. At all this the sergeant had connived and had backed up his foolish and malevolent young fascists with his own perjury. That was about the size of it, looked at in cold reality, and a rather frightening scenario it was.

Imagine how the magistrate would have responded to that kind of approach by the advocate. If he did in fact acquit, he would appear to be agreeing with exactly that view. 'And why not?' you ask.

Why not? Because the magistrates understandably cannot help wanting to favour the police. They see, case by case, day by day and year by year what an effective job the police do. They see that the vast majority of cases coming before them are properly brought. Most defendants *are* guilty, and of all crime coming before the courts 98% is disposed of by the magistrates. They are dealing with the police all the time. If they do not work on the presumption that the police are telling the truth they are as good as lost. Anyway, for the great majority of the time the police *are* telling the truth. Whatever the purist may say about the presumption of innocence, in the magistrates' courts the very human and very under- standable presumption that things are as they ought to be is the prevailing one. That is why the police tend to be believed. That is why they tend to be favoured. And that is why the magistrates are very reluctant indeed to make a finding which effectively declares the police to be scoundrels, even if that is precisely what the evidence indicates.

In the major's case the defending advocate knew what he was doing. He swallowed the truth and showed the magistrate the easy way home.

'A most unfortunate case,' he said. 'Quite clear now what had happened. Elderly gentleman wandering about at a most unlikely hour. Couple of keen young policemen anxious to keep our streets safe for the honest citizen. See him coming out of the shadows in suspicious circumstances. Mistake the defendant's peppery abuse as being that of a drunk. Understandable how mistake was made. All most unfortunate. Everybody telling the truth. Quite clear he wasn't drunk now we've heard all this impressive evidence. Magistrate indeed left with nothing to decide. Pity to have taken time of the court.'

The magistrate acquitted with a smile, gave the major his costs and everyone got out of court quickly and quietly. The client wasn't happy. He would have preferred the first kind of approach. But he was acquitted, and he might not have been if the magistrate had been pushed into the corner of having to choose whether to denigrate the police or not.

That is what 'showing the way home' is all about. Make it *easy* for the tribunal to find in your favour. Take the trouble to remove as many obstacles to that finding as you possibly can. If this means that you have to sit somewhat on what you think to be the truth, then I am afraid you will have to sit on it. If this is to be regarded by anyone as 'tricky lawyer' behaviour, that would be a pity. We live in a world of people and prejudices and our ultimate aim is to get the right result.

Consequently, it is important to remember, when making your final speech to the jury in a case where you have had to suggest police dishonesty, to emphasise this: that a verdict of not guilty does not mean that they are branding the police as liars. A criminal trial is not a balancing process where at the end you ask, 'Do we find for the police or for the defendant?'

The question to be asked is: 'Are we *sure* that we are left with no alternative?' Are we *sure* that this defendant is indeed guilty as charged?' The answer may be, 'Yes, we are, we are indeed'. In that case the verdict is guilty. If the answers are anything less than that then the verdict is not guilty. If the answer is 'I wonder', or 'I dunno. I think he did it, but I dunno', that means a not guilty verdict. Remind the jury that this is not a court where one side is claiming compensation from the other. They do not have to find either for police or defendant. A verdict for the defendant is not a verdict against the police. Get that across in cases like this and you will have removed a big obstacle to the verdict you are looking for. It is all part of the rule, 'Show them the way home'.

Eight

Judges

This is the chapter, to which reference was made earlier, about the 'anti-boot device'. What, it may be asked, is the boot? What indeed. It is the rather melancholy fact that the truly impartial judge is not necessarily in the majority in the courts of England and Wales. This may come as a surprise to those of you who have been brought up to the belief that British justice, like Rolls-Royce, is synonymous with excellence. Like all propaganda, the people who believe it don't recognise it for what it is. We have been believing our own propaganda for a long time now. British justice is the best in the world. Isn't it? The English judge is scrupulously impartial. Isn't he?

Well, you who are about to set out as young advocates will find out for yourselves. But a few gritty thoughts about the reality of what goes on in our courts may perhaps prepare your way and prevent you from crying out in disbelief when you begin to encounter what can sometimes be that reality.

Make no mistake about it. Some of the English judiciary are indeed the finest judges in the world. And appearing before one of those

excellent judges is a delightful experience. It is like playing in, or watching, a match that is faultlessly refereed. But it is far more than that. To appear in court before a wise and impartial judge who regards impartiality as his duty and who understands what the English system was really intended to be about — to appear before such a judge is a true privilege, an exhilarating experience. There is an atmosphere in the court of such a judge which is conducive to getting the right result. One feels that one is doing a good job with proper tools and with proper materials. Everything is in tune. And at the end *everybody* comes away feeling that there could have been no fairer trial, whatever the result.

Unfortunately such judges have not always been in the majority. It is gratifying to realise that things have been getting distinctly better over the dozen or so years since this chapter was first written, but many advocates feel that the really good judges are still outnumbered. So you may still find yourself before a judge who does *not* match up to the expected standards of impartiality. You have to be prepared, therefore, for what you are likely to encounter and you have to know what to do about it — in so far as anything can be done. This is what the 'anti-boot' device is all about, and in order to use it properly you need to know a little more about how some judges still fall short of the standards that our propaganda has led us to expect of them.

Let us consider, then, what we were taught to expect of the English judge. We were taught, were we not, that there are two major kinds of criminal trial — the 'inquisitorial' system that operates throughout Europe and in many other parts of the world, and the 'accusatorial' system that operates wherever the Common Law has been adopted, that is to say, in broad terms, wherever the English language is spoken? The first of these, the inquisitorial system, involves the judge taking an active part in establishing the facts, asking questions on his own initiative and frequently conducting virtually the whole of the examination of a witness before asking the *avocat* if *he* has any questions. In the accusatorial system, on the other hand, the judge acts as an impartial umpire watching over a kind of forensic tennis match played by advocates. If those advocates know their job then ideally the judge ought to be able to sit there throughout the trial saying virtually nothing.

Back in the mists of time the advice given to a new judge in England was that he should take a sip of holy water at the beginning of the day and hold it in his mouth until the end. One new appointee to the bench is said to have propped up in front of him so that he could see it at all times, a card with the clearly printed message 'Shut up'. After more than a generation on the bench one distinguished American judge still has a card where only he can see it, reading 'Be quiet'. Another story is told about a brand new judge who took his place on the bench determined to achieve such standards of self-restraint. At the end of his first day he thought he had done remarkably well and went round to his old chambers to see a friend who had been appearing in front of him all day.

'How did I do?' asked the new judge, confidently.

'Not bad at all, dear boy,' said the other. 'But you really must stop talking so much.'

It is obviously very difficult. We appoint the majority of our judges from the ranks of barristers who have been earning their living for at least the previous twenty-odd years by talking. It is no wonder that it comes so hard for them to make the change and overnight to control their inclination to intervene and to question: in a word, to talk far too much. But as the great Bacon wrote in his essay *Of Judicature*, 'An over-speaking judge is no well-tuned cymball', and the aim of our judiciary is always in theory at least to sit there in as much silence as possible, interfering only when necessary to ensure that the rules are properly complied with.

Funnily enough, some of the best judges, from this point of view, are the part-timers, the recorders who do usually no more than a month a year. It may be that this is so because they *are* part-timers and no doubt on their best behaviour. It is rare to find a recorder or a deputy circuit judge interfering too much. On the whole they provide a good example to our permanent judges. But the permanent judges, of course, have no way of seeing the recorders in action.

Returning to what we were taught to expect of our judges, and noting that comparative silence was one thing, the next and overwhelmingly important expectation was that they should be scrupulously impartial. And this is where some of them fall short. Perhaps it has always been like this: one cannot know. But without any doubt, you will sometimes encounter distinct bias on the part of many of our judges. Some of them favour the prosecution and lean against the defence. If you find this hard to believe go and talk to a barrister who divides his time between prosecuting and defending. Ask him about the differences. Making the change from defending to prosecuting has been described as being similar to the difference between riding a bicycle uphill with the wind against you and downhill with the wind behind. It is a strange and in some ways an embarrassing feeling, when turning to prosecute after a long time defending, suddenly to find that the judge is with you, that there is this helping hand coming from the bench, that the umpire is playing on your side.

There is no doubt that this is all too often so. It is not written about in the press nor discussed on the television. No Parliamentary inquiry or debate looks into the question of whether our judges are doing their job properly. There is no generally known system of inspection, no generally known system of checking on or reporting on how our judges are doing. We have no generally known committee that aims to advise anyone on whether the appointment to the bench was a good one or not. Short of a complex system that was last used in the 1700s, there is no known way of getting rid of the tyrant in the judge's seat or of making him do what he is paid to do. Once appointed, our judges are to all intents and purposes there for the rest of their working days, right up to retirement. And in the case of some of them, their retirement is awaited with impatience by all those who feel that British justice ought to be something of which we can be proud.

The fact that some of our judges are rude or impatient hardly matters. It is a system made and operated by human beings and it will be flavoured by human failings. All this can and should be put up with, for we do not live in Utopia.

But during the 1960s and 1970s there seemed to be, on the part of a number of judges a drift away from strict impartiality. It was a frightening trend and operated in this country like a silent rotting agent that undermined the foundations of our whole system. Take just one illustration of how this happened. Look at the public attitude towards the police and compare it with what our attitude towards the police used to be, say, twenty five years ago. Then there was a generally high level of respect for, and confidence in, the constabulary. Since then there has been a slow and certain erosion in this respect and confidence, such that we have seen senior policemen forced into having to defend on television their actions and those of their subordinates. The riots of 1981 shocked us all. We did not think it could happen here. The Scarman Report underlined the unhappy deterioration of relations between the police and the public that they were policing.

There have been a lot of causes for this: imbalance in communities, unemployment, prospects of a bleak future, lack of family and school discipline, apathy, the glorification of violence by the media, and many others besides. But one of the causes was this: the judges created the conditions in which the police were not only tempted but encouraged to do it the easy way, to cut corners and even to disregard the spirit of our laws. Is it generally known, one wonders, that the commonest kind of evidence offered by the police against a defendant was a confession statement, written out by the police and signed in five places by the suspect? And is it generally known that many such confession statements were signed by the defendant only after he has been held in police custody overnight without access to a friend let alone to a lawyer? Sometimes the confession statement was signed only after two nights in police custody, sometimes three.

Over and over again it was asserted by defendants that they did not make those statements voluntarily. They told of threats and bribes. They explained how they were offered deals: you confess and we won't charge your girlfriend. You confess and we'll see to it that you get bail at once. And, surely enough, when you looked into it, you found that there *was* a girlfriend arrested and taken to the police station. And when you ferreted out the records, surely enough, she *was* released half an hour after the defendant signed his confession. Again and again, in cases when the defendant said he was bribed with the offer of bail, there you found it in the record: he was released within the hour of confessing all. And as often as not, that confession was the only evidence against him.

Now you might imagine that the judges would have been reluctant to see citizens convicted on no more evidence than a confession signed after long hours in a police station, especially when it is known that no lawyer was present, no friend, no relative. Not a bit of it. Defence applications to have such confession statements excluded got turned down flat almost all the time. In went the confession, and the whole trial became an unseemly wrangle in which the police were accused of coercion and the defendant protested that he was reduced to the point where he would have signed anything just to get out of the cells.

That is what probably the majority of English criminal trials were — fights about whether the police were fair or unfair in the methods they adopted, whether, indeed, the police were to be trusted or not. And it was the jury who decided, and they acquitted by the score people who have delivered themselves trussed and bound in confessions made in police custody, setting free people who, if the confessions were genuine, must have been guilty.

We have virtually no *exclusionary rule* in England of general application, no doctrine which says that the fruit of the forbidden tree may not be used, no clear rule which declares that evidence may not be used if it has been obtained in defiance of legal protections. Until the mid-eighties, no matter how illegally the evidence may have been obtained, the judges let it in. Day after day in hundreds of courts up and down the country judges held that they were satisfied beyond all reasonable doubt that the confessions were absolutely voluntary. If an arrest was made after premises were searched, allegedly on a search warrant, judges looked askance at the advocate who demanded strict proof that any such warrant existed. Instead of making it impossible for the police to cut corners the attitude of many judges actively encouraged it. And if an overworked policeman knew that he would be allowed to get away with it, what kind of saint would he have to be not to cut a corner, not to coerce a man he thinks is guilty into making a confession, and not to bend any other rules that it might seem convenient to bend?

Happily, however, within the context of police questioning of suspects, the situation has improved. The Police and Criminal Evidence Act, 1984 — PACE — changed things for the better to a remarkable degree. Tape recording interviews removed at a stroke the bitter old wrangle about what had or had not been said by suspect *and* police. At the same time, more and more part-time judges were appointed, and, as has already been noted, the part-timers tend to be scrupulously impartial. Things have definitely been improving.

Even so, in the average criminal trial you will be interrupted far more often by the judge than by your opponent. The English judge comes down into the arena and plays, perhaps, a surprisingly active part in the proceedings. The licence that he thinks entitles him to do this is to be found in the principle that all evidence should be relevant and it is the rule, rather than the exception, to hear judges breaking in on counsel with the question, 'What is the relevance of that?'

It is difficult to answer this question because it is rarely asked in a spirit of inquiry. It usually means that the judge doesn't think your question *is* a relevant one. If you do try to explain you are thereby impeded in your cross-examination because the witness gets a nice indication of what you are doing and, if he is dishonest, he might well trim his next answers accordingly. If you don't try to explain you are left with the choice of abandoning your question and risking severe loss of status in the eyes of the jury, or of going on and appearing to ignore the judge, which would be grossly discourteous.

But it happens, and because of the general bias against the defence it happens far more to defending advocates than to prosecutors. Often the judge cannot know whether your question is relevant or not because he has not got your brief in front of him, he doesn't know what ground you are having to lay and he does not know what careful net you may be laying to expose a witness's falsehoods. But he still interrupts.

How to deal with this? Say to the judge, 'If Your Lordship would bear with me it will become clear quite soon'. That is often enough. If he goes on asking what is the relevance of your question, ask him, 'May the witness leave court while I explain, My Lord?' If he refuses you should say, 'So be it, My Lord. In the circumstances and under protest I abandon the question. I shall turn to something else.' You will probably be able to come back to it later without his objecting. If he still tries to prevent the question, go through the business again of asking to have the witness out of court. If he still refuses, say: 'Your Lordship is making it most difficult. I feel I shall have to abandon this line of cross-examination altogether.' Don't be afraid of him. He will not bite you. Be scrupulously polite but don't be afraid.

'If Your Lordship would bear with me' is a useful phrase which often succeeds in brushing aside a judge's objection. And I once heard one of the most senior advocates handle it very well. He paused, looked gravely at the judge, and said quietly, 'Your Lordship, I'm afraid, is making an already difficult case a little more difficult'. The judge kept quiet.

You cannot be given much practical advice on how to handle the unfair treatment that you will receive at the hands of some of our judges. Just keep your cool, remember that it is not necessarily you who are at fault, and reflect that as you get older in your job you will be able to handle such unfairness more and more effectively.

But the most dangerous part of the trial, the time when the judge's bias is most likely to cause damage to your case, is when the point arrives where he sums up to the jury. He has to direct them as to the law. There is no real danger there. If he gets it wrong, then the Court of Appeal will probably put him right. But after that, in England, he goes on to 'sum up the facts', and this is where our system rather tends to make a fool of itself. I say that advisedly.

If you go and sit in the Court of Appeal, Criminal Division, you will see that a very large number of appeals against conviction are based solely on the contention that the judge got it wrong or was unfair when he summed up to the jury on the facts. In the United States the judge does not sum up on the facts at all. As an impartial umpire he explains the law and refers to the facts only in so far as it may be necessary so that he can give a clear direction on how the law is to be applied. It may come as a surprise to English and Commonwealth readers to learn that in the United States part of the trial process is devoted to a debate between judge and counsel, held in the absence of the jury, to decide exactly how the jury should be directed. There are books which contain specific directions, and it will be agreed which of those directions shall be used. Before ever the judge comes to sum up to the jury there will have been an agreement between all the lawyers as to exactly what he should say. If there is any dispute, then this will have been recorded and argued through and will thus be easily available for any appeal court to consider. But in England a huge amount of time is spent by the Appeal Courts sifting through transcripts of how the trial judge summed up the facts. One wonders why we still let it happen. It is the cause of so many appeals, it wastes an awful lot of money, it uses up hours of court time and slows the whole proceedings down because the judge has to take a longhand note of all the evidence. 'Watch his Lordship's pen, Mr X' is heard in many a court-room, and the silences while the judge writes it laboriously down are silences that cost the taxpayer dear. It has been estimated that at very least 10% of the court's time would be saved if we stopped the judge summing up the facts, and that would mean a saving of, probably, several million pounds a year. Quite apart from that, a good deal of the work of the Court of Appeal would become totally unnecessary with the further saving of money that that would involve.

But far more important than this, it would remove the cause of much ill feeling, outrage and resentment on the part of accused people and their families. Nobody whose liberty is at stake is going to feel that *any* summing up on the facts is fair. However a judge puts it, no matter how scrupulously impartially he directs the jury, the accused is still going to wish that it had been more weighted in his favour and, in his frightened condition, he is likely to feel that the summing up sold him short. When, as is sometimes the case, the judge is not impartial, when the judge makes it clear to the jury that he thinks they ought to convict, the defendant's sense of having been let down by the whole system is deep, unbelieving and, to the shame of all who are involved, it is justified.

Yet the judge *does* sum up on the facts and until the law is changed on the subject you, as advocate, have to live with it. Furthermore, it is your task to do all you can to level up any imbalance which has been permitted to undermine the system of criminal justice. When the judge sums up for a conviction, he is said by lawyers to be 'putting in the boot'. It is up to you to prevent this if you possibly can and it is to this end that your final speech should sometimes include the 'anti-boot' device.

It is very simple indeed. If you have had the pleasure of a really fair trial before an impartial judge then you will have no need of it at all. But if the judge has been against you, if he has appeared to favour the prosecution and not you, then use the device. Often it makes a first-class ending to your speech, but fit it in wherever it seems best to you. Any form of words will do but say something to the jury that goes along the following lines:

Members of the Jury, there is one more thing which I have to say to you. It is this. One of the deep, solid foundations on which our system is built is the idea that the British judge is totally and utterly fair. That goes almost without saying. The impartiality of Her Majesty's judges is beyond question. When, therefore, My Lord sums up to you, as he will do quite shortly now, he will be striving to appear utterly fair, utterly impartial. But think what a difficult task that might be. Sometimes a judge's summing up sounds like another speech for the defence. Sometimes, on the other hand, it sounds like another speech for the prosecution. And sometimes it is pitched — as lawyers say — exactly 'up and down the middle'. What My Lord will now be trying to do is to achieve that perfect balance, putting both sides so that you may see them perfectly set out before you. I have said all that I have to say. Listen now while My Lord directs you on the law and seeks to put before you a totally impartial summary of the facts.

If that strikes you as a little cheeky, no doubt it is. But unhappily it is sometimes necessary. Where the boot threatens to go in do not neglect your anti-boot device.

One further comment before we leave the subject of judges. It is simply this: make it a rule to find out as much as you possibly can about every judge you appear before. If you know in advance who your judge is going to be, ask your colleagues in chambers or office for their feedback. If need be, telephone around. Look him or her up in *Who's Who*; if you can gain access to old Bar or Law Society lists, find out what chambers or partnership he or she practised in. There's no question about it that some judges warm noticeably to advocates who make reference to favourite subjects. One judge I well recall couldn't resist allusions to classical music; another positively loved references to Latin and Greek. Don't over-egg the pudding, but at the same time, don't go ignorant into the fray if you can possibly help it. We all have biases one way or another: find out whatever you can about your judge's attitudes.

If you don't know in advance what judge you are going to have, discovering this only when you get to court, then as soon as you know, ask around the robing room, then ask the usher of the court. If you are appearing before a judge you *do* know, enquire of the usher what mood the judge is in today. Such small things matter.

Nine

Note-taking

Before going any further let us very briefly consider what you ought by now to be aware of. Already you have a checklist that, written out in small lettering, you could probably get on to two sides of a post-card. Although virtually nothing has been said so far about preparation, you will before doing your first case at least have worked out with some precision what it is you want to ask the witnesses, knowing that you should never expect help from them. You will also know that, as part of your preparation, you should have worked out exactly what ground you are going to have to lay as the trial proceeds. You will know the importance of turning up to the court in good time, well groomed and wearing the right clothes. You should by now know what to call the judge, magistrate or whatever, how to ask questions and how to reply to him in the language of the court. You should know when to call people 'learned' and when not to, how to sit and stand and how not to flash unintended signals about the court-room by ill-considered or unconscious facial expressions. You should have firmly in mind the idea of being brief and economical of words and time. You should be aware of the need to keep your objections to a minimum, of the dangers of seeming to be giving evidence yourself and of how to cope with at least some of the mistakes that you are going to make.

You should have in mind all of the basic principles thus far discussed, so that you ought to be kind, adjusted to your audience, sympathetic, aiming to be the honest guide, confusing nobody, using language that everyone will understand, keeping your tribunal's attention, maintaining a level voice and, above all, not boring anybody.

Set out thus, you may feel that it presents you with something of a challenge. You would be right. There are an awful lot of things to think about at first. But if you are aware of them and particularly if you hold on to the two ideas of kindness and brevity, then you will have a head start on your fellows. Like many other things, advocacy improves with intelligent practice, and you will find that all of the desiderata set out above will become as reflex actions with time.

The rest of this short chapter is devoted to a practical topic, indeed to one of the really basic tools of your trade. Note-taking is a skill, and an important one. It is not particularly hard to acquire but you should be aware of what the objectives of note-taking are and of how a note is usually taken.

As has been mentioned earlier, because the judge sums up on fact at the end of the trial *he* tends to write down much of the evidence in longhand. He will *expect* the advocates in front of him to have been doing the same thing so that he can call for your assistance if he is not entirely sure that his own note is right. You, too, will need to know what witness A said so that you can 'put' his evidence, when necessary, to witness B. You will also need to be able to review all of the evidence that has been given so that you will know what to remind the jury of when you come to address them. You may also find that the judge gets something wrong when summing up to the jury and it is then your duty to raise the matter with him.

If you have no note you will be relying on your unassisted recollection, which is bound to be unsatisfactory. A further need for a note arises for the obvious reason that when you come to cross-examine a witness you are massively hampered if you do not have a tolerably good record of what that witness said during examination-in-chief. As a pupil or as junior counsel to a leader, the business of taking a good note may well be your most important function, providing your leader at the end of each day and at the end of the trial with the only available record of the evidence that has been given. In the United States it is possible to get transcripts in the evening of the testimony given in court during the day. That is an almost unheard-of luxury in England and happens only in the rarest of cases. Your notes, therefore, will be a working document upon which the final speech is prepared as well as a source of reference at all stages in the trial. For these reasons *you must learn to take a first-class note* and learn to do so as soon as you possibly can.

Most people do it somewhat differently but the variations are minor ones. There is an ideal way of doing it and this is what you should aim for at the outset. The 'rules' described here, if followed, ought to satisfy the needs of the more demanding Queen's Counsel or pupil master.

Use only a 'counsel's notebook'. We are lucky in the United Kingdom in being able to buy that unique and very useful form of stationery which goes under the name of 'counsel's notebook'. It is like a large school exercise book. It comes lined or unlined and with or without perforations that allow sheets to be torn out. The usual notebooks contain 48 pages and if you can afford to invest in a bulk purchase of them you can reduce the cost by up to a half.

Assume for a moment that you are about to start a ten-day defence with your pupil master. Go to court with at least two notebooks. *The first one should have every right-hand page numbered by you.* At the top of page one you should write the name of the case, together with its court number. (This is on the top right-hand side of the indictment or, in a civil case, at the top right-hand of the statement of claim and all other pleadings.) Write down the instructing solicitors' name, address and telephone number together with any reference number that may be on the papers. Note the names of all counsel, indicating whom they appear for. Note down the name of the judge who is trying the case and also the court that you are in. Your heading should look something like this:

R v William SYKES

Central Criminal Court	HH Judge C. Dickens QC 940895
Solicitors:	Grabbit and Run Barclays Bank Chambers 123 High Street SW32 (0181-234-9876) Ref: 9/1234/JK
For Defence:	J. Snooks leading A. Trollope
For Prosecution:	W. M. Thackeray leading O. Twist

Indictment:	Ct. 1	Robbery (Camera shop)	9.8.94

Ct. 2	Robbery	14.8.94
	(Jeweller's shop)	
Ct. 3	Conspiracy to Rob	1.7.94–15.8.94

You have added the briefest details of the indictment and you have thus set out, in the top half of page one, a rudimentary explanation as to the what, where, when and who of the case, together with the one telephone number that you may need in a hurry. Draw a line under that and leave the rest of the page blank. Into this blank half-page you will be able, as the trial proceeds, to keep a note of the times when the court sat, when it adjourned, what breaks were taken and so on. You will, in fact, be able to build up a complete and simple record of exactly how much time was devoted to the case, which information may come in useful at a later date, particularly when filling in any forms needed for the calculation of fees.

Make an index which starts at the top of page two. (You will note that the back of page one is left blank. It is one of the rules that *when taking a note you write only one side of the paper,* thus leaving the left hand side for comments and thoughts at a later stage.) Your index will grow as the case proceeds. You should aim to set out on page two and if necessary on the following two or three pages a record of everything that happens in the trial, so that after a while your page two could look something like this:

INDEX

p 6–8	Application by defence to sever indictment
p 8–9	Reply by prosn, and ruling. Refused.
p 9	Pleas. Jury empanelled.
p 9–15	Opening.
p 15–21	John Victimson X in Chief.
p 21–26	Victimson XX
p 27	Victimson Re X. / Peter Bloggs X in Chief.
p 30–33	Bloggs XX

The number of witnesses that there are likely to be should govern the number of pages which you allow for your index. It is no bad thing in a biggish case to start the actual note of the proceedings at page 10. At the first adjournment take the time to go through the book so far and write at the top of each page a title of what that page contains. For example, in our illustration above, page 11 would have the title 'OPENING'. Page 15 would have the title 'OPENING/VICTIMSON X in Chief; page 23 would have 'VICTIMSON XX', and so on and so forth. Keep doing this at each adjournment or whenever you get the opportunity, and your notebook will thus become a record out of which you should be able to turn up any part of the evidence at a moment's reference.

When you get to the end of the first book, number up the next one as if the pages were a continuation of the first, beginning at, probably, page 49. This makes it simpler to run your index. At the top of the front cover indicate what page numbers the book contains, and indicate which volume of notes it is, e.g. 'R v. Sykes, Vol 2, pp 49-97'.

On all right-hand pages, whether you are recording the evidence or noting down submissions, *draw a vertical margin about two inches in from the right-hand side.* Do all your noting to the left of that line and use the margin itself for comments and other notes. Leaving our example of *R v Sykes* for a moment, and assuming that you are doing a case on your own, you will use that margin as the place where you make notes relating to cross-examination or, if it is your witness whose evidence you are recording, relating to re-examination. A witness says something that you must challenge or cross-examine or re-examine about. In the margin you scribble 'challenge' or 'XX' or 'ReX' and add any thing that you think will help your memory when you come back to that part.

Coming to the note-taking itself, there is a traditional way in which this is done. You are not a shorthand writer. Even if you were you would not be able to produce a helpful note for your leader if you wrote in shorthand. It is realised that you cannot possibly get down everything that is said. A great saving on time is therefore achieved by the *telescoping of question and answer into one.* Thus:

Q   Where were you on the night of 3rd June?
A   At a party in a house in Granchester.

becomes:

  'On night 3rd June I was at party in a house in Granchester.'

In this way the note reads as if it were a narrative spoken by the witness in the first person. As the question is being asked so you are scribbling down 'On night 3rd June I was . . .', in readiness for the answer, hence saving quite a little time. If the question is 'On the night of the 3rd June were you at a party in a house near Granchester?', so, as it is being asked, you are writing 'On night 3rd June I was . . . at a party in a house nr Granchester.' If the witness's answer is 'Yes' then your note is correct as it stands. if he answers 'no' then you can easily add a 'not' after the words 'I was'.

Not only does this telescoping make it more possible for you to get down a reasonably accurate note of what is being said, it is also the way in which judges and other lawyers take their notes and this is what will be expected of you when a pupil or a junior. If you find that a patch of questions and answers simply will not allow of this kind of note-taking, then switch to as direct a record as you can manage, noting the question and noting the answer.

Interventions from the judge should be recorded as near verbatim as you can manage with the capital letter 'J' preceding the question or the comment, whichever it is. It is correctly said that the points taken by the court itself are always important, and the clearly scored 'J' will enable you later to see at a glance everything that the judge said or asked.

Note-taking needs practice. It is never easy, and a full court day where you are trying to note the entire proceedings is an exhausting process. The noting brief is a grossly underpaid enterprise. But note-taking *does* come with practice and a good and legible note is of enormous value to your pupil master or leader and many a red bag has been earned on the strength of such effort.

If you are really a star pupil/junior you will be running another, entirely separate book, in which you transcribe the most vital bits of evidence which you edit out of your main note overnight, so that at the end of the trial you have a file of the really important fragments which are likely to be of importance in the preparation of the final speech or submission.

When you come to do cases on your own, this de-luxe style note-taking will be unnecessary at first because your efforts will in all probability be confined to one- or two-hour fights in the magistrates' or in the county courts. Nevertheless, the principles remain the same even if the index is unnecessary. Always stick to the rule of one side only, always use your right-hand margin for jogging your memory and always number your pages. It makes referring back much easier. This simple methodology has worked for a long time and it continues to work.

One other thing: many barristers preserve their notebooks religiously. If you intend to do this — and there is much to be said for it — then get into the habit of marking up on the front cover the names of the cases which the book contains, together with the dates and the courts. By reference from this to your chambers' or office diary you ought to be able to find out the fullest details of every case you ever did, which will no doubt be enormously useful when you come to write your memoirs.

Ten

Endlinks and gadgets

Standing there in public, thinking on your feet, making your lone voice heard and trying at the same time to do a proper job for your client is not all that easy at first. And oddly enough, the most difficult things that the young advocate seems to encounter are the problems of how to get started, how to stop, how to round things off properly, what to do when you suddenly find that you've asked the court a direct rhetorical question, etc. This little section entitled 'Endlinks and Gadgets' is a miscellany of suggestions as to how to cope with these situations, with one or two more ideas thrown in.

Try, therefore, to think up, in advance of ever going into a court, how you are going to begin and how you are going to end. Have, in your toolbag, a little selection of handy words and phrases that you can reach for when you suddenly find that you have run out of steam a mile from the platform.

Starting is easy. Whether you are about to address the bench or to ask a question in cross-examination, a *sotto voce* 'May it please Your Honour/Your Lordship' etc. is a perfect introduction. You may certainly begin a cross-examination without such a 'May it please you', but it never does any harm. Ending seems to be where the difficulties arise so let us see what simple endlinks can be used.

There are only three things that you will want to end: an examination of a witness, a submission to the bench and a speech to the jury. At the end of the examination in chief you say, 'Thank you, Mr X: just wait there would you?' and you sit down. At the end of a cross-examination you have a choice. If so inclined you can just sit down without 'signing off' at all. A lot of advocates do this. In America one says 'No further questions' or 'Your witness', but for some reason that is never heard in English courts. You do hear 'I have no further questions' and that is a perfectly good way of ending. Another is 'Yes. Thank you, Mr X', and another: 'That's all I ask. Thank you' or: 'I think that's all I have to ask you, officer/Mrs Y. Thank you very much.' There is no magic in any of these. Don't regard ending your cross-examination as being some kind of challenge. As to your final question, we will come to that later.

When your opponent has finished cross-examining your witness you have to decide whether to re-examine or not. Again, there is a section later in this book on this topic and all that need be said here is that if you decide not to re-examine you simply say: 'I have no questions in re-examination. Unless Your Honour has any further questions?' This is the accepted way of acknowledging to the judge that you are aware of his right to question the witness and of asking him if he wants to. If the judge does ask questions he will almost always, when he has finished, ask counsel if *they* have any questions arising out of what has just been said by the witness. If you do want to take him up on that offer you say, 'If I may, Your Honour, thank you'. And you get back to questioning the witness. If you don't want to ask any questions you shake your head and say, 'Your Honour, thank you'. But when the judge has indicated that he is finished with *your* witness or that he does not want to question him at all, it is *you* who must get rid of that witness. This is when the beginner tends to show his inexperience, says 'Thank you' to the witness and sits down. This is not correct. If it is your witness in the box, you remain standing and say, 'Thank you, Mr X. Your Honour, may this witness be released?' The judge will almost invariably nod or say yes, in which case you address the witness again: 'Thank you, Mr X. You may leave court if you want to.' If the judge declines to release him, say 'Thank you, Mr X. Would you be kind enough to wait outside court?' If it is your (criminal) client who has finished then, after asking the judge if he has any questions, you say 'Thank you, Mr Sykes. Will you please go back to the dock?'

So much for how to end up with witnesses. The endlinks that can be used to finish off your submission to judge or magistrate are equally easy. The most frequently heard, and perfectly good, phrase used to sign off here is, 'Unless I can assist you further . . . ?' To which the judge or magistrate normally replies 'No, thank you' and you sit down. You can make it a little more elaborate if you wish, and it is perfectly all right to say: 'Really, sir, that is what I feel I ought to say to you. Unless there are any other matters that you would like me to deal with, I shall leave it at that.'

When ending with a jury, you can use any form of endlink that occurs to you. The 'anti-boot device' is a perfect ending. Many advocates say something like:

> Well, Members of the Jury, that is what I want to say to you. There are many other points I could have dealt with but it is quite unnecessary for me to go over everything: you heard the evidence and it is your decision. Thank you for the patience and the attention with which you have listened to me.

Something along these lines is all you need: all manner of variations will occur to you, so work out half a dozen for yourself and learn by heart at least two or three of them. It is remarkable how helpful it can be if you have in your memory just a small handful of endlinks, literally learned verbatim. Don't intone them like some kind of litany: say them as if they were coming out for the first time. If you have a few familiar props that you can lean on, you may find it helpful in your early days.

So much for starting and stopping. Let us look briefly now at the rhetorical question and the scourge of parenthesis.

The word 'rhetorical' comes from the Greek word *rhetor,* which simply means orator. Oratory and rhetoric are not what advocacy is about, not these days anyway, and the kind of approach that you hear in the debating societies and in the university unions tends more towards rhetoric than advocacy. Since it is in the debating societies and unions that the law student usually gains such experience as he has of public speaking he will find, no doubt, that the change of style may be a little difficult at the outset. The one thing which characterises rhetoric more than anything else perhaps is the unanswered question, or the question flung out by the speaker and then answered. 'What has this government done about the problem of such and such? Nothing!! And why has nothing been done about this fundamental and desperate problem? Because this government are a load of incompetent time-servers!!' It is great for debating and political platform speaking but when you come to a court of law, use it with absolutely infinite care.

Make no mistake: it does have its use. But it is enormously dangerous and this is why a little time is being devoted to it here. Follow this rule: the rhetorical question *may* be used before juries but *never* before the Court of Appeal, the single judge or the stipendiary magistrate. For safety's sake don't use it before the lay magistrates either. Confine it to juries. Like all rules, this one can be broken but try to follow the rules until you know them before experimenting with modifications. The reason why you should never use the rhetorical question before the judges, the professional lawyers, is that they do not like feeling that you are in any way haranguing them. If, therefore, you find that you are there, on your feet, before a professional judge, and despite your trying to follow the rule, out pops a nice plump rhetorical question, what do you do about it?

You neutralise it forthwith. By the time that it is half-way out you will realise what you have done. Finish the question and as soon as you have, add on the throwaway phrase 'I ask it rhetorically, of course', and on you go. This indicates to the judge that you are perfectly well aware of the fact that you are not supposed to harangue him and tells him that you are not intending to do anything of the kind.

This illustrates another, very general rule that might be stated thus: it is to your considerable advantage if you can *convey to your court that you know the rules,* that you know the form and that you know what is expected of you. The judges and stipendiary magistrates have to tolerate so much amateurism on the part of advocates in their courts. They who have a lifetime's experience of advocacy themselves have to try to sit silent while the same obvious mistakes and illustrations of incompetence are trotted out before them *ad nauseam* by inexperienced and often apparently thoughtless beginners. If you think about it, it must be horrendously trying on their patience. If, therefore, when you, a totally unfamiliar face, turn up in court, the judge or magistrate may be forgiven for suspecting that here is yet another incompetent.

It will come as a pleasant surprise to him to find any evidence that you seem to know what you are about. Any phrase that you use to indicate that you know something about advocacy is bound to do you good. That first crisp 'May it please you, sir' coming from a properly dressed, properly groomed stranger who has been sitting properly in court until called on, gets you off to the right start. Questions asked properly in your first cross-examination will continue the drift of sympathy in your favour. Your brevity will again indicate that you appear to know your job. Indeed, by the time you have been on your feet for as short a time as five minutes you ought to have been able to mark yourself out as someone who knows at least some of the rules of the game, and this will incline the court to listen to you with relief.

One of the things that tries the patience of almost all professional judges is time-wasting. Even if you are *not* wasting time the judge may very well express his impatience at having to sit there, doing what for him is this tedious case, by interrupting with the words 'Do let's get on!' It can be very off-putting to have your judge do that. Yet it can be avoided and you can at the same time convey to the judge that you know about the need not to waste time simply by throwing in to your examination or cross-examination from time to time the sentence: 'Well, we must get on: I shall leave that'. Then turn to something else. It is astonishing to see in our major courts even senior advocates indulging in long pauses in their cross-examinations while they visibly think where to go next, and what next to ask the witness. When this happens one can see the judge's impatience grow, one can see him exercising self-control. If, therefore, you need time to think, pick up a document, look at it and say, 'Would Your Lordship bear with me for a moment?' This conveys to the judge that you know that continuity is important, and that time is valuable, and you get all the time you need to think without losing any of your status in his eyes. Since the judges have come to expect so much non-professional-ism before them, these little 'gadgets' used by you will indicate that, beginner though you may be, you are not a thoughtless or ignorant one.

Returning to the rhetorical question, as has been said already it *can* be used before juries.

'And what did X have to say about that, Members of the Jury? Well, let's look at the explanation he offered.'

'What would you have expected then, Members of the Jury?'

'And why did that happen? Well, we heard about that, didn't we?'

But use it with caution. Remember that you ought to be talking to them rather than making a speech and remember that the rhetorical question is essentially an orator's gadget, not an advocate's.

Now, parenthesis. Used properly it can be very effective. A little aside thrown into the main body of your sentence can add colour and variety. But using parenthesis properly is very difficult. What is so often heard is the beginning of a sentence interrupted by another, later, idea that has just occurred to the speaker. A third of the way through his second idea another one occurs to him and off he goes on to that. The whole thing starts to sound like a pageful of unfinished thoughts and can be difficult to listen to, let alone to understand. It has to be controlled. Some people are more afflicted by the tendency to parenthesise than others. Try to discover whether you are one of those afflicted and if you are, work to reduce the habit. If you find that you continue to drift into parenthesis then, when you are before a professional court, make it a bit less irritating for the judge or magistrate by acknowledging what you are doing.

You find that a new thought occurs to you as you are half-way through expressing the old one. If you really must break in with this new thought then use some such phrase as '. . . and if I could interpolate here. . .', and go on with the new idea. Like the phrase, 'I ask it rhetorically, of course', it is a kind of apology for appearing to depart from the ideal way of doing things. It is a message to the judge or magistrate that you do in fact know the ideal and that you are either intentionally departing from it or knowingly not quite achieving it. If the court sees that you are not departing from the ideal because you are unaware of what that ideal is or ought to be, you should retain the court's respect. If you let the court get the idea that you just don't know what the ideal way of doing it is, then you run the serious risk of causing irritation, and that does nothing but harm. But if you can manage it, your aim ought to be to avoid parenthesis altogether except on rare occasions and then with the specific intention of using it for a purpose.

Just two more things and this chapter is ended. First, Cicero. It was said earlier that one of his techniques is alive and well and living in the courts today. Let me describe the gadget and leave it to you to decide whether you think it honest, whether you want to use it. What it amounts to is this. You can say a lot of things in court by protesting that you are *not* going to say them. You can emphasise a great many things by saying that you are going to ignore them. It is a sub-variant of the rule that everything has its equal and opposite. Example:

I am not going to refer in this final speech to the bad character of the accused which, as you know, is marred by convictions stretching back for the last twenty years. I pass by without mention the fact that this is his thirteenth appearance in court charged with burglary in the last five years. I shall not invite you to consider . . . etc. etc.

It is an ancient, ancient technique of advocacy, *the assertion of the opposite*. 'I come to bury Caesar, not to praise him.' Rubbish, Mark Antony! It certainly works. But to my mind it smacks just a little of 'the clever lawyer'. Anyway, there it is described: it could hardly be omitted from a handbook on advocacy. Decide for yourself if you want to use it.

PART TWO

THE EXAMINATION OF WITNESSES

Eleven

Questioning

There has been at least one entire book devoted just to the art of cross-examination. Francis Wellman wrote it in the United States at the turn of the century. It is still available though not easily so, and it is still to be recommended highly. But despite all that you have heard about cross-examination and despite the drama that it often engenders, it is not at first the most difficult of the three kinds of examination of witnesses. For the beginner it is in one sense the easiest. There are comparatively few technicalities that have to be understood and you are not likely to be left speechless, in cross-examination, felled by just not knowing how on earth to cope, as you might well be in examination in chief. Most people can brandish a sabre. What they do with it is a different matter. But it takes a little learning to handle a scalpel, and this, in a sense, is the difference between cross-examination and examination in chief, at least at the outset.

As to the third kind of examination, re-examination, this is one of the most neglected areas of advocacy, much overlooked and little understood. But woe betide if you find yourself up against an opponent who has made a real study of the subject and who has turned re-examining into the sinister art-form that it can be.

We will deal with each of the forms in turn. But first some considerations that are general to all three. There is in the majority of courts of

first instance a court-writer, taking everything down verbatim either in shorthand or on a stenography machine. If necessary a transcript can be prepared of the whole proceedings and sometimes is. Seeing yourself in transcript is often an unnerving and embarrassing experience, somewhat akin to hearing yourself for the first time on a tape-recorder. 'Did I really say that?' you wonder, squirming. You did indeed, and seeing yourself in transcript is far more often a cause for dissatisfaction than for self-congratulation. This is when those of you who are afflicted by undisciplined parentheses see it all, coldly staring back at you, peppered with the shorthand writer's struggling attempts to punctuate your ramblings. This is where your garbled questions and fishings for answers are laid out for you to reflect uncomfortably upon, preferably in some quiet and private place.

Now remember that shorthand writer. Remember that that dreadful record is quietly being made and that some misfortune could call it into solid existence, page after page of you, yes you, on your feet in one of our courts of law. Think about it. Be chastened and remember the potential transcript. If you do then there is at least a likelihood that your advocacy will become a bit more taut, your questions a bit better judged and your contentions on law a bit more closely structured.

And bearing that transcript in mind aim for this ideal. You won't always achieve it but aim for it: *try to make all your questions occupy not more than one line of transcript each.* That means not more than about ten words. Have that line of transcript somewhere in your mind and aim not to exceed it. You will be amazed how often you really can achieve it if you try, and it is one of the secret pleasures of advocacy, aiming for and achieving these private objectives.

Stripping your questions down to that compact size will automatically take care of a common problem, that of the composite question. If you permit a question to ramble on you may very well find that you have asked two questions instead of one, and the judge may well intervene by asking, 'Which one would you like the witness to answer?'

It seems too obvious to need stating but it is a very common beginner's mistake, so have in mind the cardinal rule to *ask only one question at a time.* If you are confining your question to a maximum of a dozen or so words you will hardly be likely to offend against the obvious and basic 'one at a time' rule. You will also get into the habit of working out exactly what it is you actually want to ask. You will break down your inquiry into a series of sub-questions and you will find that by simplifying in this way you will make for much greater clarity of thought on your part and greater ease of understanding on the part of judge and jury. You will also find that if you make your questions very short they will more often allow of a yes or no answer. This has its advantages in cross-examination because you are able to direct the witness into giving the evidence you require far more easily in this way than by any other method. The short question tends to get a short answer and the succinct question-and-answer is a much more manageable building block than the gargantuan monoliths that are so often encountered in our courts.

So hold on to that transcript. Even when you clearly have to abandon the objective and spread your question over four or five lines you will nevertheless be aware of the space you are using and you will not become prodigal. Remember what was said earlier about thinking of the court's time as ticking away on a taximeter that you are going to have to pay for. Think of the space you take on the transcript in the same way. Not only will this attitude of mind lead you to greater brevity: it will also lead to precision, and *precision is what the examination of witnesses ought to be about.*

So, one line of transcript and one question at a time. What other generalities should be stated? Clearly your question should be just that, a question. Make sure it is. Beginners often make statements at witnesses, hoping that an upturn in the voice at the end will make all come right. *Get into the habit of formulating questions as questions.* If you need to make a short statement as a preamble to your question, so as to place it in context or to make it comprehensible, then take care that your short statement is indeed short. If you go on too much with a preamble to a question the judge is likely to accuse you of giving evidence. If he does then back down at once: 'Your Lordship's quite right, of course. I'm sorry. Let me try again.'

There will be, both in examination in chief and in cross-examination, a number of questions which it is not easy to formulate while standing there in court. It is no bad idea, therefore, to work them out in advance and jot them down in your notes. Some advocates write out entire examinations, so that every question they intend to ask is there in front of them. The majority, however, take the view that this is too limiting. If you are trying to stick to a pre-planned pattern you may well find that you are sacrificing far too much in the way of flexibility. It is all very well as long as you get the answers that you are expecting, but if the witness suddenly departs from what you anticipated you may very well find that you are wrong-footed by the conflicting inclinations of sticking to your plan on the one hand and going off on the new line that the unexpected answer has opened up on the other. The more favoured view appears to be that writing out an entire examination is both unnecessary and hampering. Rather, have a list of *topics* that must be covered, and here and there in your list, have written out any question that you feel may be difficult to word in the heat of the moment.

It is surprising how many advocates start an examination without any very clear plan in their minds as to where they are hoping to go. This is rank unprofessionalism. Before you rise to examine, cross-examine or re-examine a witness you ought to be in such a position that if some magic intruder came in, suspended time and asked you exactly what you had in mind for this particular witness, you would have no hesitation in explaining it to him, briefly and clearly, there and then.

Hence, *know your objectives with every witness.* Define them for yourself in advance. Make a note of those objectives if it helps you. Indeed you might find it helpful to make a point of doing this at the outset of your career and keep doing it until the exercise has become totally automatic. This again makes for succinctness; it also makes for the appearance of efficiency. If you know exactly where you are aiming to go, your examination is likely to appear, and indeed to be, purposeful. And, it cannot be repeated too often, if you appear to know your job you will not lose the sympathy of the court — not for that reason, anyhow.

It is sometimes offered as a maxim of examining witnesses that you *should never ask a question to which you do not know the answer.* This is a bit of an over-simplification; it is the statement of an ideal in much the same way as the 'one line of transcript' rule is. But what it means is this: taking a blind leap into the dark is never a happy thing to do. If it becomes utterly and absolutely necessary, then so be it; but if you can avoid getting into the position where you are obliged to take a blind leap so much the better. The experienced and skilful advocate never finds himself forced into that position. He plans his questions and arranges his direction in such a way that the need for the blind leap does not arise. It is, in a way, an offshoot of the old proverb about fools rushing in where angels fear to tread. If you go gently and test the ground ahead of you with tentative questions you ought to realise when you are walking into quicksand. And having realised that that is what you have done, do not suddenly draw back with a start, thus signalling to the whole court that you think yourself on dangerous ground. You remain absolutely calm and just change the subject: 'I see. Well, let's turn to something else.' If you approach your topics by short questions, you ought to be able to assess the kind of progress that you are making. You ought to be able to see your way ahead at least clearly enough to be alerted to danger. This is what is really meant by the maxim 'never pose a question to which you don't know the answer'. It is closely related to the maxim about the fatal final question, but we shall come to that when dealing with cross-examination.

Before turning to the first of the three kinds of examination, let us consider one much misunderstood thing, the *leading question*. Most of you no doubt understand exactly what is and what is not a leading question, but since it is the subject of such ill-informed usage a few illustrations might be helpful so as to eliminate any possible misunderstanding.

The layman, when asked, 'What were you doing on the night of June 3rd?' may well answer, if he for any reason feels that he is being asked to reveal something significant, 'Now that's a leading question!' In fact it is nothing of the kind. On the contrary, it is a perfect illustration of what is *not* a leading question. It matters nothing that the question calls for information that the witness would rather not reveal. It is not the answer called for, but the form of the question that determines whether it is leading or not. Simply defined, a leading question is one which contains its own answer, one in which the advocate *puts words into the witness's mouth*. So, 'Where were you on the night of June 3rd?' cannot be leading, but if the question were, 'On the night of June 3rd were you standing outside the Inner Temple library?' then it would be.

Another illustration: 'You told the inspector that you had just parked the car, didn't you?' That is a leading question. It contains its own answer.

'Is your date of birth the 9th of August 1936?' is another.

'When were you born?' while inviting in strictest and amusing technicality a breach of the hearsay rule, is not a leading question.

'Do you live at 99 Theberton Street, Islington?' is leading. 'Where do you live?' is not.

'Is that enough about leading questions?' Well, work that one out for yourself!

Now, three more general points and then we can come to specifics. First, *remember what has already been said in this book about not expecting help from witnesses.* Treat all your own witnesses as being potentially foolish, as being dumbly willing to let you down if given the chance, and as being in need at all times of your unobtrusive guiding hand. Second, *try to conduct your examinations in such a way as to make them sound as conversational as you can.* Remember the general rule about being as kind as you can at all times. Conduct all your examinations in a spirit of inquiry and listen to the answers with quiet interest. Nothing is more conducive to boredom throughout the court than the sight and sound of an advocate intoning his way through routine evidence, looking and sounding as if he is stifling yawns. So many do it, however, that the actors have picked it up and made the languidly disinterested advocate a stock caricature. Don't become a model for caricature yourself. By short questions eliciting short answers you can make the examination easy and conversational.

And third, *develop the habit of riding the bumps.* This is important. Briefly referred to earlier, it is a variant or extension of the rule about knowing what your face is doing, about not flashing unintended messages about the court-room.

If you ski you ought to understand the analogy. Watching an expert skier one sees that head and shoulders tend to remain in the same position relative to the ground, while the knees are bending and flexing incessantly, absorbing the bumps and adjusting for the irregularities of the terrain. The general image is one of a smooth and often swift gliding motion, but a glance at the knees shows that this glide is achieved by a lot of skilled and automatic work by thigh and knee. It is the same in a well designed car. Over rough roads the body travels smoothly enough, with the pot-holes and ruts being accommodated by the shock-absorbers. In the same way it is essential that the tyro advocate develops — and develops as quickly as possible — an ability to ride the bumps, so that even if he hits the most awful rut or jars into the most dreadful pot-hole, the smooth glide of his progress does not appear to be disturbed.

The examination of witnesses is rarely a smooth ride for the questioner. But it must be made to appear so. Every examination has its pot-holes and ruts but the skilled advocate is not seen to lurch into the one and to trip over the other. Smooth progress is the impression that you are aiming to give, for if you appear to be flustered or winded or thrown off balance this is likely to do inordinate harm to your client's case. You have to maintain your status. If, as you should be, you are trusted by the jury then they cannot help but be deeply affected if they see you, the 'honest guide', suddenly stumble and fall or, even worse, if they see you turn pale and begin to tremble.

If you think about it, it comes down to this: you get what you believe to be a shockingly damaging answer. You may be right in your belief: you very probably are. But if you respond with any indication of your belief then you are interjecting *your opinion* into the case. And that is bound to be improper. Quite apart from anything else your opinion may be wrong.

Let us consider briefly the three kinds of examination. The advocate who calls a witness either examines him in chief or, in certain limited circumstances, asks the witness no questions but 'tenders' him, putting him into the witness box and making him available for his opponent to cross-examine. By the act of putting a witness into the witness box the advocate, whether he examines in chief or just tenders, offers him for cross-examination by his opponent. When the cross-examination is over then the advocate who called the witness may, if he wants to, re-examine on any matters which arise out of the cross-examination. In England it is a three-stage process: examination in chief, cross-examination and re-examination. If the judge asks questions at the end he may ask counsel if they want to ask any further questions as a result of what the witness has just said. And if either advocate has forgotten to deal with something then, with the judge's permission, he may have another go. But in principle it is a three-stage affair. In the United States this limitation does not necessarily apply, and the examination in most jurisdictions can continue on the basis of 'direct', 'cross', 're-direct', 're-cross' and so on until everyone is content that everything has been elicited from the witness.

The rules as to questioning are simple enough. You may not ask leading questions of your own witness. Thus, no leading questions in examination in chief or in re-examination. (There are a few exceptions to this and we deal with them later.) But if you are examining a witness whom *you did not call*, then any questions that you ask are asked in cross-examination, and you are free, if you wish, to ask leading questions. Bear these simple rules in mind and you will have no difficulty in knowing what kind of questions you may ask.

I remember the first time I appeared robed in court. I was briefed — if that is the right word — to do a judgment summons at Wandsworth County Court where the smell of cooking hops in the brewery next door was all pervading. I asked my fellow pupils how to do it. A very important chap, all of six months my senior in call, said, 'You just cross-examine him and ask him how much he spends on cigarettes and beer every week.' And I was truly confused, wondering how I could 'cross-examine' him who hadn't been called as a witness by somebody who had taken him through his evidence in chief. Had I applied the above rules — had I known them even — I would have realised that anyone in the witness box whom I had not called and whom I was invited to or entitled to question was being exposed to my cross-examination. Hence, if you find yourself defending one of several defendants in a multi-handed fight, remember that you are entitled to cross-examine all of the prosecution witnesses, all of the other defendants who give evidence and all of the witnesses whom other advocates call.

Enough then by way of introduction. Let us now come to the first kind of examination of witnesses.

Twelve

Examination in chief

Here again, great changes have come about in England and Wales. Examination in chief has become, at least in civil cases, an endangered species of British advocacy. This is because, in the early 1980s, the commercial judges and the official referees started suggesting to litigants that they should exchange witness statements: it was believed this would remove the element of surprise, save time, and facilitate settlement. This exchange of witness statement quickly came to be seen as a substitute for live evidence in chief. 'We have his statement. We know exactly what he would say in chief. Let's get straight on with the cross-examination.' To quote a senior member of the Bar Council: 'With bewildering speed, the witness-statement procedure was taken up by the Rules Committee as a panacea and, within six years, the entire English civil tradition of live evidence in chief was virtually ended.' It is now commonplace for judges to *order* an exchange of witness statements, and to insist that such statements shall stand as the examination in chief.

This fundamental change was designed to speed things up and cut down on the cost of litigation but, predictably, it has had the opposite result. Witness statements now have to be comprehensive and some of them run to as many as twenty thousand words. The time which lawyers have to devote to preparation and 'polishing' of such statements has added to the costs of litigation, and placed the rich litigant at an even greater advantage over the poor one. Far more paper is generated, and cross-examinations have tended to become longer. 'It is a paradox, curious but true, that the shift from oral to paper presentation has not only increased the cost of trial preparation but has also increased the length of trials themselves.' Whether there will be a return to the more efficient, time-hallowed, oral examination in chief in civil disputes remains to be seen. In criminal cases, however, it is still done the old-fashioned way, and you must know how to do it.

The difficulty that you are faced with here is that save for very limited exceptions you have to get the witness to tell his story, give his evidence and testify as to the facts that you have called him to prove, without asking him leading questions. This takes a certain amount of practice. If you are dealing with a non-professional witness, particularly one who has literally never given evidence before, then you may well find that he simply cannot work out what you want him to say. You are not allowed to explain to him what you want him to say, you are not allowed to put words into his mouth and you must be infinitely careful not to 'lead' him on any matter which might conceivably be in dispute. How, then, is it done?

It is done by bearing in mind the 'one line of transcript' rule, breaking the thing down into the shortest questions eliciting the shortest answers, and by analysing out as you go along what building bricks you in fact require in order to erect the structure of evidence that you want from this witness. Broken down into the smallest pieces, every story, just about, can be drawn out of a witness without leading questions being used. But you often do have to break the narrative down very finely.

Let me illustrate in very simple terms. Take the wedding of the Prince of Wales in July of 1981. Unfortunate though the outcome of that marriage may have been, its setting still provides an excellent illustration for the purposes of examination in chief. Imagine that you are seeking to adduce evidence from a witness who sat in St Paul's Cathedral as to what happened there. We will assume that your opponent is not disputing the month and year when this happened. The questions and answers might go something like this:

Q   Where were you in July of 1981?
A   What do you mean where was I? I was in lots of places.
Q   Very well, tell us where you were in the second half of that month?
A   I was in Australia, then in India and then in England.
Q   Do you remember the date when you arrived in England?
A   Not exactly. It was a few days before the 29th.
Q   That will do. Tell us, why do you remember the 29th?
A   It was the wedding of the Prince of Wales: everybody knows that.
Q   No doubt they do, Mr X. Where were you on that day?
A   I was actually at the Cathedral.

Q   For which part of the day?
A   The morning: I was a guest at the wedding.
Q   Forgive me for seeming very stupid, Mr X, but I need *you* to tell us for the record. Which cathedral?
A   St Paul's, of course!
Q   In London?
A   Where else?
Q   Thank you. And can you remember what time you arrived there that morning.?
A   About 9.30.
Q   As a guest were you seated or standing?
A   Seated, of course.
Q   Facing the altar, on which side of the aisle were you seated?
A   The left side.
Q   About how many rows back from the front row?
A   About 20, I suppose.
Q   And how many seats in from the aisle approximately?
A   Five or six. I didn't count.

So far, and without (save for the month and year) any leading questions, and with a somewhat impatient witness, you have in about a page of transcript narrowed down the location of your witness from anywhere on the surface of the planet Earth to a fairly exact placing on the left of the aisle in St Paul's Cathedral, London, where he was sitting after 9.30 on the morning of the 29th July 1981. It is a very simple illustration but it demonstrates how it can be done. Break it down into tiny bits. To go on:

Q   Were you present during the actual wedding?
A   Of course, that's why I was there.
Q   Did you see people standing at the altar?
A   Of course I did.
Q   Are you able to tell us now whom you saw?
A   The Prince of Wales, his brother Prince Andrew, Lady Diana, her father and the Archbishop of Canterbury.
Q   Did you see any of those people arrive at the altar?
A   Apart from the Archbishop, I saw them all arrive.
Q   Are you able to say in what order they arrived?
A   I think so.
Q   Would you be kind enough to tell us who arrived first?

A The Princes.

Q Are you able to say what time that was?

A I'm not, as a matter of fact.

Q Very well. Who arrived after the Princes?

A The bride and her father.

Q Can you say approximately how long the Princes had been waiting before the bride arrived beside them?

A About five minutes, I think.

And so on and so forth. You will notice that even here there has been a borderline question. 'Did you see people standing at the altar?' is in one sense a leading question. But except with the strictest judge or the most difficult opponent such a question would not be objected to because it saves time and because in the context of what you have already established the matter cannot have been in dispute. This is the test of when *you may ask leading questions of your own witnesses: when the matter either is not or could not conceivably be in dispute.* Check with your opponent as to whether you may lead on those parts of your witness's evidence that you think are not in dispute. He may be quite happy for you to lead. He may indeed interrupt your examination in chief, if you haven't checked with him, with the interjection, 'This is not disputed, My Lord: my friend can lead the witness if he likes'. If you have checked and if your opponent has agreed, then indicate to the judge that you know what the rules are and that you are not asking leading questions because you do not know any better. Say, before you ask your first leading questions: 'My friend has kindly said I may lead, My Lord'.

Get into the habit, though, of asking as few leading questions as possible. Remember that if the words come from the witness himself rather than from you their impact on the judge and/or jury tends to be much greater. If, therefore, you can get the evidence you want without the use of leading questions, do so. This is particularly to be borne in mind in cross-examination. Get into the habit of asking the witness to give his own name and address. Make sure you know what they are so that if he speaks too quietly to be heard easily you can repeat them aloud. Bear in mind that the judge and shorthand writer will be recording these details: if either name or address contain anything that is unfamiliar it is a courtesy on your part to spell that bit out loud.

Coming back to the Royal Wedding, you noticed that we led the witness on the month and year: 'Where were you in July of 1981?' It was not in the strict sense a leading question because it did not contain its own answer, nor did it put words into the witness's mouth. But it did introduce into his evidence the month and the year of the incident that we were intending to ask him about. By telling us where he was then he effectively adopted our timing: *facts came from the advocate and not from the witness*. Let us stay with this point for a moment so as to make its importance quite clear. Surely, you may be thinking, the date of the wedding was known to half the population of the world? How can it be improper to 'lead' the witness on that? Answer your question with another one: how reliable would you think that witness to be, if, soon after the event, he had been *unable to* recall that unbelievably well known date? Much stranger things happen in court, and it is on such unlikely points of detail that the credibility or otherwise of many a witness is demonstrated.

Consequently it is essential that you should understand and apply the rule that *the factual content of your witness's evidence must not come from you*. Do remember that. In chief or in re-examination it is vitally important for you to frame all questions in such a way as to avoid giving your witness any of the facts which should be coming from him. Once you have done it, you can't take back the factual information that is now out there, flapping around the court-room. No matter how enthusiastically your facts are adopted by your witness, they nevertheless came from you in the first place and it is too late to do anything about it. Not only does it diminish the value of the witness's evidence; but also it could be that, without your prompting, the witness would never have given that evidence at all. You may have deprived your opponent of a totally fair opportunity of showing how unreliable your witness was. And if the matter is an important issue in the case your mistakes may well have gone a long way to nullifying the whole process of the trial. Conceivably your opponent may apply to have the jury discharged and for the trial to begin all over again. And the judge may allow it. Ignorance or carelessness on your part may waste hundreds and perhaps even thousands of pounds of taxpayers' money. That is why this lesson is of vital importance.

When a witness is called by you, your opponent is always entitled to require you not to lead on any point at all. He can demand the strictest observance of the rules, conceding nothing. If you have a witness whom the other side suspect of being about to perjure himself or of having learned just the salient facts of his evidence or even of being just plain unreliable, then your opponent would be doing less than his duty by his client if he did not say: 'Give him no help at all. Let's see just what he can remember and tell us without any prompting whatever.' So be scrupulous in understanding this rule and in taking the utmost care to apply it.

Sometimes it can be very difficult to do, and it may take a certain amount of ingenuity on your part to examine in chief without ever prompting your witness as to facts. This is why examination in chief is so hard for the beginner and why it so cruelly marks off the amateur from the professional. It takes practice to get an account from a witness without once helping him on the facts, and it is much to be recommended that you get together with your fellows and treat this challenge as a sort of game. Practise extracting information from each other in short questions without any prompting. Get used to going round the houses if you have to. But practise with each other. Most of us did it the hard way, finding out about the difficulties of examination in chief when on our feet in court, examining our first ever witness.

How on earth do you begin at all if your opponent demands total adherence to the rules? What kind of introduction can you use? Your witness is sworn and you have asked him his name and address. Where do you go from there? You can't say, 'Where were you in July 1981?' You want him to talk about the wedding. So how do you start?

Q Mr X, do you recall a recent and much publicised event?
A Do you mean the Royal Wedding.
Q If you please. Do you have any particular reason for remembering the Royal Wedding?
A I was a guest.
Q For the sake of the record would you help me with a few details? Can you recall the month of the wedding?
A July 1981.
Q Do you recall the exact date?
A Wasn't it on the 29th?

In an ordinary case where you have been asked by your opponent not to lead at all, you may find that you simply cannot think how to begin.

You cannot put the date to the witness, not even the year. You cannot put the place of any incident nor can you lead on names. You have to get started somehow. Begin by declaring your difficulty: 'My friend has asked me not to lead in the slightest way'. This at least tells the judge that you are not being intentionally awkward and if he has any humanity it will invoke his professional sympathy. You can then go on:

Q Mr X, can you tell us, please, why, do *you* understand, have you been asked to come to court today?
A To give evidence.
Q Quite so. Would you tell us please what *you* understand you've come to give evidence about?
A It's about that car crash, isn't it?
Q Do you remember a particular car crash?
A Yes.
Q Where was that crash?
A In the High Road.
Q The High Road where?
A Woolwich.

You are away. You can now inquire about all the details. An alternative starter might be: 'Are you acquainted with anybody in this court-room?' followed up by 'Do you recall a particular incident in which Mr Y was involved?' Or again: 'Do you recall an incident about which you are able to tell us?' To which the answer might be: 'Yes, I think so', allowing you to proceed, 'Just tell us then, in your own words, what happened'.

But do it all with confidence. Do not appear at a loss. The jury don't know that this is not the normal way of doing it. The judge should in the circumstances be sympathetic. Approach it in as many ways as you have to in order to get your witness started. Even the most obtuse will get the message after three or four such nudges. Do not get impatient. If you appear irritated this will convey that something is not as it ought to be, and you do not want to give that impression.

Once you have the witness started, keep it as conversational as you can. Short questions and short answers. Try not to interrupt your witness's replies. If you do it sounds as if you may possibly be wanting to stifle some of his evidence. If he wanders too much, then *let* him wander a bit before interrupting, so that the judge and jury can see you are only doing it to help. Thereafter you can interrupt him, within limits, in order to keep him on course. Sometimes you have a really good witness who needs very little help. If you are confident that he is all right on his own then intrude as few questions and interruptions as possible. Let him tell his story for himself. If the flow gets going you may find that all you have to say from time to time is 'Go on, please', or 'And what happened then?'

Some advocates take the view, already referred to, that if your witness is up to it, it is best to ask as few questions as possible in chief, and let him tell the tale as uninterrupted by you as possible. There is a lot to be said for this, but before you give your witness such free rein be satisfied that he has got the attention of the court and that his account is in fact coming out smoothly.

If you choose to conduct an examination in chief in this manner, letting the witness tell the tale with as few interruptions from you as possible, you will find that *some* judges step in and take over the examination themselves. If this happens to you, recognise at once that with *this* particular judge you cannot adopt the just-tell-us-what-happened approach. Take back full control of the witness at once, with or without apology to the judge, aim for short questions calling for short answers and keep your witnesses on a tighter rein from that point on.

When examining your client, the defendant, do not neglect giving him the chance to deny his guilt. It is a good, effective way to finish up in chief by asking him the stark question: 'Did you do this thing that they accuse you of?' or 'Are you guilty or not guilty of this crime?' His denial, upon his oath, carries weight. If you have prepared your jury properly to expect your client to be cut about in cross-examination, that simple affirmation, by him, of his innocence as his cross-examination is about to begin, can be slightly heroic.

Before finishing, make sure that you have covered all the points that you should have covered. Except by leave of the judge (which you don't want to ask for since it makes you look amateurish) you will not get another chance to ask your witness questions until re-examination, and then you must confine those questions to matters which 'arise out of the cross-examination'. Therefore, as part of your 'homework' you should always prepare a skeleton list of the topics and, if necessary, of the major heads of detail of matters that you will have to deal with in chief.

One thing you will have noticed, no doubt, is that the rule against leading questions is waived when you are seeking to elicit a denial from your own witness. 'Were you at 3 Kings Bench Walk on the night of 3rd of June?' 'No.' It could hardly be otherwise.

So much for the hidden difficulties of examination in chief.

Thirteen

The basic approach to cross-examination

Introduction

Let me begin by making one thing quite clear. This book is intended to be a guide for the beginner — a survival manual, if you like, for the young advocate. It does not aim to teach the art of advocacy. It hardly touches on the craft. It is a book about the basic materials of the trade and how to use them. I emphasise this here because cross-examination is a very personal skill. There are certainly wrong ways of doing it but there are very many right ways of cross-examining, all of them very different. For this reason alone it would be presumptuous of any practising advocate to say: 'This is how to do it.' He would effectively be saying: 'This is how *I* do it. Follow me.'

Not only do I refuse to do that, but virtually all other practitioners would refuse as well, and for this reason: when we get to our feet to cross-examine, we all wonder if we are going to be up to it. I do not think there is any lawyer in the Kingdom, sensitive enough to be a good advocate, who rises to cross-examination without wondering how he will make out this time. I know famous silks of the highest ability who tremble as they begin. So when you rise, dry-mouthed, to cross-examine, remember that. Nobody knows how well or badly he or she is going to do. It is the great leveller.

Consequently this section of the book will concentrate more on what not to do as much as on anything else. If you want guidance on the way that successful cross-examiners have operated in the past then go to *Art of Cross-examination* by Francis Wellman (Collier-Macmillan, 1962) and to *The Art of the Advocate* by Richard Du Cann (Penguin,

3rd edition, 1982). Read the memoirs of the great advocates. Read the reports of famous trials. Above all, go to courts as often as you can and listen. The hints that are given in this book are of general application only, but it is hoped that they will save you from the worst of the blunders that you might otherwise make. You will find, in the beginning, that cross-examination can often be an exhausting, uphill struggle. For years I kept asking myself in court, 'Why did they brief me? Why didn't they get a real barrister?' Yet one day, about five years or so in, I noticed that it had been some time since I had had a really tough time in cross-examining; it had been quite a while since the inside of the wig prickled so uncomfortably and the collar had seemed so hot. It was good old-fashioned experience making itself useful at last. It will be so with you. But knowing what not to do should help both you and your clients during the years when you are gaining experience.

Hold on to this thought. There is far too much cross-examining done in our courts. The first and most important question that you should ask yourself is: *do I need to cross-examine at all?* If the answer to that is really no, then be firm with yourself and don't yield. Say 'No questions, My Lord' without fully getting to your feet.

The next thing to ask yourself and to keep asking yourself as you cross-examine is: have I got enough? *Can I sit down yet?* The questions set out in this paragraph should be engraved in your awareness: you should be conscious of them at all times.

It is said that most cases win or lose themselves. The old (and exaggerated) adage goes that ninety per cent of cases are unaffected by advocacy. Five per cent are lost by bad advocacy, three per cent are won by good advocacy and two per cent are totally wild. Cases that are lost by bad advocacy are often enough lost by bad cross-examination, and more often than not bad cross-examination means unnecessary cross-examination. Don't forget that every time you ask a question you are playing with a Pandora's box. You are taking a risk.

If the risk is justified, all well and good. But the number of unjustifiable risks, i.e. quite unnecessary questions, that one hears in our courts is really quite shameful. Often those unnecessary questions are asked quite mindlessly. It is as if the advocate feels that he won't have earned his fee unless he cross-examines for some given stretch of time. Again, quite often you see a cross-examiner carried away with enthusiasm. He has got what he wants or needs but he can't resist trying to underline the fact. He goes on. He asks that one question too many, that unnecessary, fatal question too many.

A very endearing anecdote was told by a now famous High Court judge at an Oxford college law dinner some years ago. It was a story against himself when, as a very young barrister, he was defending two villains on a charge of attempted burglary. The prosecution said that in the small hours of the morning and in the silent emptiness of a town square a police sergeant had come upon the villains trying to break into the local jeweller's shop. He had approached, so he said in chief, to within twelve feet of where they were trying to pick the lock or whatever. Of course, the cross-examination was an attack on the sergeant, designed to show that it was utterly impossible for anyone, let alone him, to have got so close to the burglars without their noticing his approach. And the questions went something like this:

Q   Sergeant, would you be kind enough to tell us how tall you are?
A   Six foot three, sir.
Q   And no weakling! Would you mind telling us your weight?
A   Tip the scales at just under twenty-three stone, sir.
Q   That night — wearing uniform, were you?
A   Yes, sir.
Q   Helmet?
A   Yes, sir.
Q   Greatcoat?
A   Tunic, actually, sir.
Q   Boots?
A   Yes, sir.
Q   Regulation issue boots, sergeant?
A   Yes, sir.
Q   What size were they?
A   Size twelve, sir.
Q   Yes, I see. Size twelve boots, Studded with hobnails, were they, like the normal regulation issue?

A   (Pause) Yes, sir.

Q   They had a kind of small horseshoe of metal on each heel?

A   Er, yes, sir.

Q   And you say that you approached to within twelve feet of these men without their seeming to notice your arrival, sergeant?

A   (Pause) . . . Yes, sir.

Q   In a totally empty square at two in the morning?

A   (Pause) . . . Yes, sir.

Q   Nobody else around was there?

A   No, sir.

Q   Normal flagged pavements were there?

A   (Pause) . . . Yes, sir.

Q   I mean, you didn't approach over a lawn or grass of some kind, did you?

A   (Pause) No, sir

(Enough? Impossible in the circumstances to believe that the sergeant could have got up to the villains, who had normal hearing, without being heard? Time to sit down? One question too many coming up.)

Q   Well, really, sergeant, can you suggest to the magistrates how you could possibly have got as close as you say you did without being heard by the defendants?

A   On my bicycle, sir.

The point could hardly be better emphasised, could it? And do not assume that the sergeant would have volunteered that he was on his bicycle. Witnesses are often not intelligent enough to fill in the gaps in their own evidence. Nor should you assume that the prosecuting barrister or solicitor would necessarily have been able to put it right in re-examination. It is quite possible that he simply did not know that his witness had been using a bicycle that night. But for that fatal final question the matter might well have rested there and by the rules of our trial process it would hardly have been open to the prosecution, as the defence made their final submissions, to bring the sergeant back to testify further, this time as to his bicycle. Remember, too, that although you are hoping, as an advocate, to be contributing to the discovery of truth, we nevertheless operate, as has been emphasised before, in an adversary system. It's not your job to do the other side's work for them. By the fatal final question you often do just that. So how do you avoid taking that risk?

Try to understand what the real, the ultimate purpose of cross-examination is. It is to elicit evidence: it is not to make comment as you go along. If you get the evidence out of the witness, you have achieved your objective. It is much later in the trial that the time comes to comment on that evidence.

Keep those two functions clearly separated in your mind: getting the evidence and commenting on its implications.   In the bicycling policeman illustration that fatal final question was really a comment and not a question at all. It was intended to say: 'There. Get out of that one if you can!' It was a comment which said: 'In all these circumstances that I have now elicited evidence about, it is not possible that the sergeant has got it right'. That comment could, and should, have been made in the final speech. Instead it was enthusiastically made as a flourishing end to what had otherwise been an excellent cross-examination. And everything fell apart.

That final question was dangerous for another reason. It relinquished control of the witness and gave him full rein, effectively, to say whatever he wanted to say. Until then, you notice, the questions had complied beautifully with the 'one line of transcript' rule. They had been short and simple and had kept tight control over where the evidence was going. But suddenly all those commendable objectives were abandoned. The sergeant was offered the chance, if he wanted to, of saying whatever he wanted to say. A mistake in cross-examination is often a mistake for more than one reason. Let us therefore try to formulate some basic rules which, if followed, will help to keep you out of trouble. We have dealt with a number of rules of general application, so all that is needed next is a recapitulation. What rules have we got already? There are nine of them, divided into three groups, which might be conveniently thought of as 'general', specific' and 'cautionary'.

General rules

1   Be as kind as you can.   This is something you should have been aiming for throughout the trial. If you get the jury thinking, 'Thank

God he's not cross-examining me', you will, as has already been emphasised, lose their sympathy and divert it towards the witness. If the time comes when you do have to get nasty with a witness (and that time does come now and again), then the contrast between the nice you and the nasty you will not operate against you.

I watched a co-defending barrister in pre-PACE days conduct his entire case with sweetness and light, turning away almost all of the evidence with smiles and admissions. He stripped the prosecution case down to its bare essentials and showed, by so doing, that it was mostly composed of conjecture and inference. Just one witness stood out. A detective sergeant said that the defendant had admitted all, not in writing, just in a cell interview. None of the suspect's rights had been given to him, no solicitor's visit, no telephone call. The barrister began as gently as he had with all the other witnesses. But the detective sergeant didn't like the 'short question, short answer' method. He began making speeches. Suddenly the advocate was quite different. Half-way through the second answer he broke in, 'Officer!'

A   Sir?
Q   Been in the police force long?
A   Fifteen years.
Q   Given evidence before?
A   Many times.
Q   Capable of understanding a simple question are you?
A   Yes.
Q   I'll repeat my last question.

He did. It was a one-liner, quite easily understood and in all fairness it required a yes or no answer. The policeman raised his voice and started to make another speech. The barrister gave him half a dozen words and then said briskly: 'Do stop messing us about, will you. It's a straight question. Give me a straight answer if you know how!'

And everyone agreed with him, judge and jury alike. This nice chap who had gained everybody's sympathy because he *was* a nice chap and who was regarded as an honest guide had snapped into action against the witness with a few terse phrases of homely slang that everybody understood. The witness *was* messing us about, and we all wondered how he had messed the suspect about in the cell. The witness backed off and the barrister whipped through his necessary challenges as contemptuously as I have heard it done. He ended up with the words 'That's all', and sat down. His opponent wisely didn't try to repair irreparable damage. The witness left court, cheeks burning, and not long after that his defendant was acquitted.

You are entitled to hit hard sometimes, to be unpleasant. But if your nastiness is utterly the exception rather than the rule then it will work *for* you. Do understand that some advocates take the view that the tough approach from first to last is the right method. With some of them it works. Sir Patrick Hastings was a tremendously famous and successful advocate whose ethic was to terrify the witness with his first question and to slam into him all the way through. Even for him this didn't always work and for the beginner it is almost certainly a recipe for disaster. You will discover soon enough what your strengths are and when is the right time to show your teeth. At the outset stick to being as nice as you can even if, as happened to me in pupillage, your solicitor pokes you in the back just as you are fearfully getting to your feet to cross-examine and hisses, 'Maul him!'

2 *Ask your questions in a spirit of inquiry.*   This general rule is very similar to the first one. Almost all witnesses under cross-examination expect to be attacked and a gentle and inquiring approach will counter this. They will ease up and relax somewhat and be far more likely to agree with the version that you put forward than they will if they feel under hostile pressure. And very often what you are trying to do in cross-examination is not flatly to contradict a witness but to persuade him to change his viewpoint.

Memory is a funny thing: we all tend to round off the awkward corners of recollection and in all honesty and quite subconsciously to 'remember' the version that 'feels' most comfortable. For intellectually minded people this often means that their memories subconsciously erode off the bits that don't rationally fit into the picture. For the less intellectual they 'forget' the bits that don't 'feel' easy to explain. Very few recollections are really accurate and once you have gently shown a witness that with the best will in the world he *can't* have remembered one particular bit correctly, then he is quite likely to go along with you when you suggest that he might have been wrong on other bits.

Do not forget that in the criminal trial, when the burden of proof demands that before convicting the jury must feel *sure,* all that the defending advocate has to do is to raise reasonable doubt. If you have a witness eventually saying: 'Well, I thought I was certain but now we've had this chat about it I'm not so sure after all', there's your doubt. You are far more likely to get there by sympathetic inquiry than by hostile confrontation.

3 Expect no help from the witness. This is a familiar rule and is always to be borne in mind but especially, and obviously, so in cross-examination. Oddly enough many cross-examiners plunge in without plan or caution and go off on that well-known beginner's adventure, the 'fishing trip'. They seem to think that they might get something useful if they just cast about, seeing what turns up. Most of the time they fish out old boots and bicycle tyres. Sometimes they find that they've hooked and landed something much bigger and nastier than they are equipped to handle. Whether you get boots and tyres or the ugliest pike in the pond it does you no good. Boots and tyres make you look foolish. Pike have a nasty bite.

This leads on to another rule which can conveniently be stated here. *You must aim to have a specific purpose to every question,* and not appear to be asking questions that do not have a specific purpose. If you do appear thus then you will inevitably lose credibility in the eyes of judge and jury. If your court is left wondering 'Why did he ask that?' then you must leave them looking forward to finding out the answer. If you seem to be asking questions that do not have a purpose they will lose interest, and quickly. Another way of expressing this rule is by saying: *try not to appear to fail in anything that you do.* It is a variant of the rule about riding the bumps and for all these reasons the fishing trip is to be discouraged. Apart from anything else it is very quickly recognisable for what it is, it is one of the badges of the bad advocate, it wastes time and it quite justifiably drives some judges frantic.

Specific rules

4 Stick to the 'one line' question as much as you can. In cross-examination this is even more important than it is in chief. It enables you far more easily to 'guide' the evidence and to keep a tight rein on the witness. And keep asking short questions which allow specific and short answers. If you ask a witness 'Why did you do that?' you are inviting a long reply. If you are willing to take the risk of getting an unguided and uncontrolled reply then do it by all means. But bear in mind the risk. Work out for yourself what kinds of questions invite the limited answer and which the uncontrolled. 'Why?' is clearly dangerous. 'Exactly when?' is safe.

5 *Avoid the multiple question.* This is almost too obvious to need restating but it is important to ask only one question at a time.

6 *Aim for precision.* Aim for exactness in your questions. Mentally break down what it is you are after. Analyse out exactly what it is you want to do with your question. Practise the skill for fun in vacant moments. The edges of your questions should be clean cut. If you get into the habit of asking non-woolly questions you are likely to achieve non-woolly thinking processes. The two very much go hand in hand.

Now let us come briefly to the restatement of the 'cautionary rules'.

Cautionary rules

7 *Don't ask the question to which you don't know the answer.* It has already been emphasised that this way of stating the rule is a bit misleading, but it is put in this way because the advice is an old cliché of advocacy. It means, more realistically, that you should tread carefully, looking before you leap, not rushing in blindly and being aware that you may be entering a minefield. We do not often, in everyday life, come on a situation when we do not know where our next step will land us. There is hardly any need for this in cross-examination either. If you know where you are trying to go then you should have some fairly clear idea of the terrain ahead of you: when you come to really uncertain bits go very gently. If you think ahead you rarely find yourself having to ask a question totally blind. When you do it is a horrible sensation that really does bring a feeling to your throat that makes you understand the expression about having your heart in your mouth. So unless you can see where you are going, go inch by inch. But take care not to make it appear that you have slowed right down. Keep your tone inquiring and business-like. Seem interested in the answers. You will know quite soon if it is safe to proceed. If it is not, back off, but remember the next rule.

8 Do not suddenly draw back with a start. If your foot touches a mine or starts to sink into the quicksand draw back gently. Ask a question with all matter-of-factness about some topic that you have just dealt with. Go back and ask a totally unnecessary question to get a bit more detail on something that the witness has already talked about. If you can, ask a question to which the witness is likely to reply 'Sorry, I don't know'. To that you can say, 'Very well, let's turn to something else'. You are out of trouble and never by a flicker have you signalled to anybody that you may even have been in trouble in the first place.

In truth, you may not have been, and if you neglected to conceal your anxiety you may very well have raised a totally unfounded suspicion on everybody's part. Again it should be emphasised, this acting cool, this advocate's technique of not appearing anxious when he is, is not some kind of dishonesty, some conjuring trick. It is one of the tools of your trade, to be used to avoid misleading your court. And, of course, it is a subdivision of the last of the recapitulated rules.

9 Ride the bumps. This advice has already been discussed at some length and need not be repeated here. One hint, however, is perhaps worth passing on. What you do to maintain your unruffled appearance when you get a simply crucifying answer is ultimately a matter for you. But an old 'trick', that has been used for centuries no doubt, is to write that answer down. Look as if you welcome it. 'Aha,' you say. 'Just a moment, Mr X. Let me see if I've got that right.' And write it down, repeating it word for word as you go. Read it back to the witness: 'Is that right?' 'Yes.' 'Good. Well then, let's turn to something else.' And with the calmest demeanour do just that. With all that has been said in this book about honesty that 'trick' may strike you as a bit slippery, and it very possibly is. But it is as old as the hills and could hardly have been left out of a basic manual such as this is. With appropriate excuses, therefore, there it is.

The mandatory rule of putting your case

So much then for the recapitulated general rules. We come now to one very specific matter which you simply must understand because it is a mandatory rule in England and Wales. It is the rule that in cross-examination you have to 'put your case'. In our courts we work on this principle: when you have an adverse witness in the box and you know that you will be calling evidence at a later stage about something material that the witness said or did, then it is regarded as completely unfair if you don't give this witness the opportunity of having *his* say on the subject. So if Smith is in the witness box, with you cross-examining him, and Smith has said something that you do not accept because what he says conflicts with what your witness, Jones, is going to say later on, then you must give him the chance of making his comment on what Jones is going to say.

Thus, if Smith, the adverse witness, says that at 9.30 p.m. he was in the Blue Coat Boy, drinking pints, when he saw X come into the public bar in the company of Y, and you know that you have a witness, Jones, and another one, Robinson, both of whom are going to testify that at 9.30 p.m. Smith was in Chingford, then it is your *duty* to suggest to Smith that he was not in the Blue Coat Boy and that he was in Chingford at the material time. You have to 'put' your version to the witness. The same is true when half a dozen police officers testify that your client said such and such and did so and so. If your client denies that, then you must put it to the police officers that they have got it wrong. If your client says 'I said not what they say, but this, this and this', then you must put to these witnesses that your client said this, this and this. The fact that you will get a whole series of answers 'No, he didn't sir, he said what I've already testified he did', is irrelevant. The rule is that you must put your case to the witnesses who are giving evidence that conflicts with your case.

This is where the expression 'I put it to you' comes from. 'I have to put it to you, Mr Smith, that far from being in the Blue Coat Boy at 9.30 p.m. as you have told us, you were in fact in Chingford at the time.' There is no magic in the words 'I put it to you'. They have almost become a cliché and like most clichés ought to be used sparingly and avoided if possible. As long as you understand what you are supposed to be doing then any form of words will do perfectly well.

'You weren't in the Blue Coat Boy at 9.30 p.m., were you, Mr Smith?'
'Yes, I was.'
'Weren't you at Chingford at that time?'
'No, I most certainly wasn't.'
'I hear what you say. Did you not meet with Mr Jones and Mr Robinson at that time?'

'No, I didn't.'

That is quite enough. Or you could say:

> 'I suggest you weren't in the Blue Coat Boy at 9.30 p.m. but in Chingford.'
> 'No.'
> 'And I suggest you saw Jones and Robinson there.'
> 'No.'

You haven't used the words 'I put' at all but you have definitely 'put your case' to the witness.

A moment's thought about this rule ought to make you realise one vital thing about advocacy in the English courts. Since your duty is to put to the unfriendly witnesses any challenges you have to their evidence this means that you simply must know, and must have at your absolute fingertips, exactly what your client and your witnesses are going to say. There is no short cut to this. Before you begin the trial you must have got into your mind every salient point of your client's version of the case and of his supporting witnesses' evidence. You must know what parts of the prosecution evidence will have to be challenged so that you will be able to put your version to the witnesses as one by one they give evidence.

This is not easy. It requires practice and organisation. It requires a very clear understanding of your own case and the carrying of quite a number of facts in your mind. If you slip up and fail to put a material challenge and your client in giving evidence later makes that challenge himself, both prosecutor and judge are likely to say, 'That wasn't put'. They are dreadful words for a defending advocate to hear spoken, because they mean either that he has been negligent or that his client is making up his evidence as he goes along.

Think about the second half of that alternative. In the Crown Court, the prosecution let the defence have all the statements of the witnesses they propose to call, well in advance. If, half-way through a trial, they want to call an extra witness they will have to serve a notice on the defence, setting out exactly what this extra witness is going to say; and if the defence need time to consider this new statement the judge will grant them an adjournment so that they can do just that. Because the defence are told, in advance, what the individual prosecution witnesses are going to say, there is no excuse if the defence lawyers do not go through every line of the statements and find out what bits, according to their client, are disputed. This is what they are expected to do. It is their duty. They are *presumed* to have done it. They are presumed to know what is challenged, and by the time the defendant comes to give evidence it is presumed that everything which is in dispute will have been put to the prosecution witnesses.

If, therefore, the client, when giving his evidence, raises a brand new challenge, this can mean only one of three things: either the defence lawyers did not go through the statements properly with their client, or the defending advocate forgot to put the matter, or the client is making up his evidence — concocting it in the witness box. The first two alternatives are presumed not to be the explanation since it is assumed that the lawyers are not negligent. It is therefore presumed that the client is concocting his evidence.

If it is your inefficiency that was the cause you can imagine how you will feel as you see your hapless client accused of making it up, of lying. And do note: it is not sympathetically received by judge or opponent if you try to remedy the situation by rising, red-faced, and explaining that it was your ineptitude that led to this. Your ineptitude may have meant that the whole picture of the case has been improperly coloured. If the prosecutor had known that this bit *was* challenged, he might have gone about the case quite differently, asking different questions, perhaps organising extra witnesses and planning his strategy in a thoroughly different way. It is like asking, eight or nine goes later, to be allowed to take back a chess move. It is rather disgraceful, in fact. Consequently, if you do nothing else right at the outset of your career, do please learn to do this properly.

One thing you may have noticed about putting your case is that you often have to abandon the 'one line' principle. You obviously cannot stick to the 'very short question and answer' if you are having to tell a witness what you suggest so as to invite his comment on it. You should, nevertheless, be aware of how much transcript you are taking up as you put your case, because such being aware is likely to make you as economical as possible. Continue to think as analytically as you can: continue to break things down into the smallest bits that you can conveniently accomplish, and *aim* at all times for the 'one liner' ideal.

Although this rule about having to put your case is, as has been strongly emphasised, a mandatory rule that you must observe, it is not entirely burdensome for the cross-examiner. It carries with it quite a lot of advantages. If, for instance, you are about to cross-examine a witness and you can think of no way at all in which you might be able to undermine his evidence, then putting your case at least gives you something to do.

I watched a trial once in which the defending advocate did literally nothing else. He did not try to show that the recollection of the several witnesses was faulty. He did not try to show that they were telling stories which were inconsistent with each other. He did not accuse anybody of lying. Again and again, with more than half a dozen witnesses, he just put his client's version of events. He did it with aplomb and assurance. And it was interesting to observe that as he kept repeating his client's version, everybody in court, having heard it again and again, began to feel as if his version had at least as much validity as the version being put forward by the prosecution. At the end of the prosecution case he put his client in the witness box, and, on his oath, *he* told us the now familiar story. When he was cross-examined he stuck to that story, and by the time that four or five witnesses called by the defence had repeated the same thing the jury had heard it so many times that they obviously felt they could not reject it. The client was acquitted.

If at the beginning of your career as an advocate you feel understandably nervous about what to ask your witness in cross-examination and about how to 'break' his evidence, remember that comfortable 'staff' of putting your case. If you have nothing else to lean on, lean on this. You will be surprised at the other ideas that occur to you as you do it.

But one thing must be emphasised. Nothing is worse than putting your case in a manner which seems and sounds weak. One sees some truly pathetic examples of this in our courts. Young advocates tentatively suggest to experienced police witnesses that they have got it wrong and that such and such happened instead.

'No sir,' comes back the indignant reply.

'Oh', says the young advocate, and shuffles his papers, looking for the next thing that he has got to put. 'Well I suggest so and so . . .', again apologetically, tentatively.

'No sir', again.

If it is done in this gentle, rather hopeless way, then the 'No sirs' come like hammer blows, driving nails into your client's coffin, and you lose your status, your credibility and your case.

Do it confidently. Do it as if you believe it. Do it briskly. Be business-like. Know exactly what your client's version is: do your homework and prepare any necessary notes so that you never have to delay. As one denial comes from the witness, so be ready with your next challenge, your next bit that must be put. Go steadily and inexorably through your version. If you permit yourself to appear woolly or tentative in this or unsure of the version you are putting forward then you are letting yourself and your client down. There is no reason why you should be, because this part of your cross-examination is capable of the most minute preparation in advance.

One thing you should note. Most judges are willing — relieved even — to let you put your case to the first available witness and then to ignore the others. If you want to take advantage of this you ought to say to the judge when the corroborating witness comes to be cross-examined: 'My Lord, I've put my case at length to Detective Sergeant X. Unless Your Lordship or my friend feels I should do it all over again I don't propose to cross-examine this witness'. This usually leads to the judge's grateful rejoinder: 'So be it, Mr Snooks'.

A few words and phrases that might help you in this part of cross-examination are easily borne in mind. The phrase 'I hear what you say' is magnificently neutral but it carries the overwhelming implication that you don't believe a word of it: 'I hear what you say. Next I suggest that . . .'. Do not overdo it. It is an endlink, and endlinks ought to be varied. 'Very well' is another useful one: 'Very well. Let me now come to. . .'. Or:

Q   That's what you say, is it?
A   Yes.
Q   I see. Let me come to the Tuesday. I suggest that . . .

One last hint about putting your case. It is always a good idea to go through the other side's witness statements with your client and as much in advance of the trial as you can. In pencil you can put a line of ticks above those parts of the statements which are not to be challenged and can put a line of crosses over those bits which are disputed. Often you can write your client's version in the margin and thus work merely from one document while on your feet. If this is not possible then you clearly have to work from two documents, the unfriendly witness statements and your own client's comments on them. But the ideal that you should ultimately be aiming for is to know your client's version so well that you can put your case without referring to any document at all. One famous advocate from the past had the astonishing reputation of never opening his papers in court. The ribbon remained untied throughout, yet he could deal with every question thrown at him. 'Your Lordship will find that in the second bundle at page 234 in the third paragraph, My Lord . . . . ' That, of course, was pure virtuosity but as an ideal to aim for it is worth recording. So much for putting your case.

Go back now to chapter 5 and re-read what was said there about *laying the foundation* for any comments you want to make to the jury at the end of the trial. Much foundation laying has to be done in cross-examination and this section would be incomplete without reference to this other mandatory requirement. But enough has been said on the subject and for the sake of brevity it is not repeated here.

Fourteen

The objectives of cross-examination

We come now to a matter which was touched on in chapter 11 and could well have been dealt with at the very outset of these chapters on cross-examination, so vitally important is it. But you may appreciate these remarks more easily now that you have a few guidelines under your belt. It is this. Before ever beginning a cross-examination, before ever deciding whether you even need to cross-examine, you must *decide what you are hoping to achieve.* Ask yourself, in fact, 'What is my objective with this witness?' As in so many other things, cross-examiners often plunge in without ever considering this, and such thoughtlessness borders on lunacy. One of the first things that an officer-cadet is taught on his induction into the army is the simple concept of military thinking: 'What is my objective? What resources do I have available with which to attain that objective? What losses can I afford to sustain?' Those straightforward questions (which admittedly may not allow of anything other than the most agonisingly complex answers) indicate at the outset a system of clear thinking which is as commendable as it ought to be obvious. And so it should be with all cross-examination. What are you trying to achieve with any witness? Know this before ever getting to your feet. Let us consider what, in general terms, cross-examination might hope to accomplish.

There are four broad objectives. Each cross-examination will have at least one of these as its aim. They are:

(a) *Laying the foundation* This has been explained in detail already.
(b) *Putting your case* has also been covered in depth, so there is no need to elaborate further on either of these. The third is somewhat related to the first and may be described as:

(c)   *Eliciting extra and useful facts*   which go to support part of your case. If, as you go along, you have the chance of getting confirmation from the other side's witnesses of something which you know is part of your case, then it would be silly to pass up the opportunity of getting that confirmation. Consider, though, before doing this, whether the matter which you are thinking of getting confirmed is something which is really in dispute. If it is, then take this opportunity with every available witness if you can do it safely. If it is not really in dispute then touch on the matter with just one adverse witness and leave it at that. The next heading is the big one.

(d)   *Discrediting the evidence.*   Let us pause here for a moment's reflection on the true nature of a court-room trial. As has been mentioned earlier, *it is not a procedure which is aiming to find out the truth.* If that sounds astonishing, just think for a minute.

All manner of limitations are imposed on the process. There are rules of evidence designed to exclude all sorts of proof which may help considerably in arriving at the truth. That excluded evidence may well lead straight to the truth of exactly what happened. It is excluded because, for one reason or another, it is thought to be unfair or unsafe.

A suspect may make a really genuine confession to an investigator in which he gives complicated details. The details are only capable of being known by the suspect if he was indeed the culprit. The more that his confession statement is checked the more it becomes utterly clear that what he has been saying is the truth. In his statement he names names. He tells the investigator who his associates were. He describes in detail the parts that they played. His account bears all the hallmarks of truth in *this* regard as it bore all the way through.

But no matter how genuinely true his statement may be proved to have been in every other particular, that statement is not and cannot be evidence against the associates that he has named, unless he made his statement *in the presence* of those associates. If he did, then the statement is admissible as evidence against the associate in whose presence the statement was made. Why? Because if the denunciation was made in the presence of that associate he had the opportunity there and then of refuting the allegation. If he did not refute it, then the allegation and the associate's failure to refute are admissible. But if the associate was not there at all, the statement is not evidence against him. It is not thought to be fair and it is accordingly excluded.

Even a palpably accurate statement may be rejected as evidence against the very person who made it. If the judge decides that it was made only as the result of a threat or of an inducement and that it was not made voluntarily, out it goes.

These are just two examples of the way in which evidence that may be totally reliable is kept out. Again, all the rules against hearsay are said to be based primarily on the fact that the person who spoke the words reported by another cannot himself be cross-examined. For this reason, excellent and perhaps totally truthful and accurate evidence is just not used. It is not thought to be safe.

One could go on. A lot of what may well be perfectly good evidence is kept out because it is felt that there is a risk of it being unsafe or unfair. As Lord Devlin said, the jury is not a committee of inquiry. Neither, indeed, is the single judge. In the adversary system it is up to the party who asserts something to 'prove' it to be the case. The jury are not going to step in with advice on how they would like something to be proved. The judge may comment that he is dissatisfied with the standard to which something has been 'proved' but, except very rarely, he does not regard it as his job to order that new kinds of proof be brought before him. Neither judge when sitting alone nor jury are there to find out what the truth is. In criminal trials they are there to answer this question: on the evidence that has been presented, and in some cases on the absence of evidence that we would have expected to be presented, are we sure or less than sure that X did what is alleged? In civil trials the question is different: on the evidence adduced and/or on the absence of it, is it more probable that what X asserts is right or is Y's account more probable?

This is in no sense hair-splitting. In all trials we go on the evidence and ask what that evidence adds up to. In criminal trials, does it add up to being sure of guilt? In civil trials, does it make us feel that one version is more probable than the other? It is important to bear this in mind at all times.

One hears judges and prosecuting counsel tell jurors that it is up to them to decide where the truth lies. This is not correct. It is both woolly

thinking and cliché on their part. It is for the jury to decide whether
the *evidence* has convinced them to the point when they are sure, or in
civil cases for judge (and in the United States frequently and in
England very occasionally, the jury) to decide which version, on the
evidence, is more probable.

Discrediting the evidence

When you come to cross-examine you must have this in mind, because
it reminds you at all times of a very important distinction. When you
try to discredit the evidence of an adverse witness it is exactly *that* that
you are trying to do. *You are seeking to discredit the evidence of the
witness, not the witness himself.*

With that distinction clearly understood, you will realise that there are,
of course, occasions when the best apparent way to discredit the
evidence is to discredit the witness himself. If you are able to show
that he is in fact a liar and that he is lying on this occasion you are
clearly discrediting him personally, but that is not your principal
objective. If you can show that he is biased towards your opponent's
side, or that he is utterly foolish to the point of unreliability, or that he
is suffering from some illness that affects his understanding, or that he
has a lot to lose by giving a different version, then although you are in
a sense discrediting the witness himself, your objective and indeed
your attainment has been to discredit the evidence.

In general terms how might you go about discrediting the evidence?
Here I propose what might be thought of as the *'discomforts rule'*.
Think first what it is that you are trying to do: to demonstrate that the
evidence is not safe to rely upon. For what reason might it be unsafe?
*Why might you personally feel unhappy about relying on it totally if it
were you who were being asked to take some important personal
decision on the strength of that evidence?* If you ask yourself that
question you will very probably find that a number of things occur to
you: the weak points in the evidence will tend to make themselves
obvious.

Take the simple example of the sergeant on the bicycle, narrated
earlier. As you sit there in court, listening to him give his account and
wondering if you personally would find it convincing, it at once leaps

out at you that any policeman approaching a couple of burglars in the silence of the night was likely to have been heard. His footsteps must surely have been audible. This, then, is the intrinsic weakness in his account and it is to this that the cross-examiner is likely to turn.

A very much more experienced advocate would no doubt have thought it through to the end. He might have said to himself, 'Here is the weak point in this evidence. This is the bit that I would feel uncomfortable about if it were I personally who had to take a decision on the account given by this witness.' But he might also have gone on thus: 'Let me assume, though, that the witness is honest, and let me see if there is any way in which he could have approached those two burglars without their hearing him. How might he have done it?' At once he is casting about in his mind, wondering how it might have happened. Rubber soles on his boots, perhaps? Approached along a grass verge perhaps? How else might it conceivably have been done? Took his boots off? Unlikely. Walked on tiptoe? Ludicrous. When you know the answer, of course, it is obvious. A bicycle can be as silent as a ghost.

The barrister in question eliminated everything apart from the bicycle and designed his cross-examination accordingly. And well he did it. But he had not thought hard enough. He had not tried hard enough to explain the apparent weakness in the evidence. If he had managed to think it all the way through and had hit on the idea of the bicycle then what should he have done? He would have had a choice. He could either have faced it straight away:

Q Were you on foot that night or on a bicycle?
A Bicycle, sir.
Q I see. What time did you say this all took place?

and so on. It would have been found out by this first question that the apparent weakness in the evidence was not a weakness at all. He might therefore have abandoned that entire line of cross-examination.

He might, on the other hand, have decided to take the risk. Anticipating what the final answer might be, he could well have pursued his cross-examination right up to the point of establishing that here was a hobnailed twenty-stone policeman approaching in the silent square *and left it there,* taking the risk that his opponent just did not know and did not have the gumption to guess that the officer might have been on a bicycle, and hoping that it would not come out in re-examination.

Whichever way he dealt with it, he would have been *ready*. You may therefore find it helpful, when wondering how to approach a cross-examination, to follow the kind of thought process outlined above. Do a sort of cockpit check by asking yourself the following questions:

(a) If I personally had to act on this evidence are there any bits that would leave me feeling uncomfortable? If so, what are they?
(b) If I personally had to act on this evidence is there anything about the witness that would leave me feeling uncomfortable? If so, what is it?
(c) Assuming that the evidence is infact completely reliable, how might my various discomforts be explained?

When you have worked out the discomforts and their possible explanations, then put them to the witness. Do it in a spirit of inquiry. Eliminate those explanations that have occurred to you, one by one. If one of them turns out, in fact, to be the explanation then you have discovered, without any loss of status, that this is not a weak point in the evidence after all. You can turn to something else. If, on the other hand, you run right through your list of possible explanations you will have discovered that this very probably *is* a weak point, and at the appropriate stage you will be able to make much of this when you come to comment to the jury or the judge. It goes without saying that you should avoid the fatal final question, 'Well how then . . . ?' It is comment, and you might get a bicycle thrown at you.

This 'discomforts rule', as I have called it, is only a suggested way of approaching cross-examination, but you may well find that it helps you to identify the 'discreditable' parts of the evidence and shows you how to test those parts without committing yourself, stumbling and losing status. Apply this approach to any evidence in chief. Take the police witness, for instance, who testifies that the suspect verbally confessed all in a police cell. That is all — there is no other evidence, no fingerprints, no written confession statement under caution, no contemporaneous notes, no independent identification, nothing at all. The context of this example is, happily, less likely since the arrival of PACE, but such situations can still occur and the illustration is still a useful one.

Now if you personally had to act on that evidence these absences might cause you discomfort. Look at the discomforts. See if you can think up possible explanations for them? Fingerprints can be avoided by gloves.

Q   Did he have a pair of gloves with him when arrested, officer?
A   No, sir.
Q   Searched his house, did you?
A   Yes, sir.
Q   Any gloves found there?
A   No, sir.
Q   Any gloves found at the scene of the crime?
A   No, sir.
Q   The place was examined for fingerprints, was it?
A   Yes, sir.

Q   Were my client's fingerprints found there?
A   No, sir.

You would have heard about it in the opening if prints *had* been found and in the Crown Court you would have been served with written evidence to that effect, so that final question involved no risk. And you have made the very valid point that there were no 'dabs' on the scene and that your client apparently had no gloves. Certainly he could have thrown a pair of gloves away after committing the crime but you cannot get everything. You have examined your first 'discomfort' and scored a perfectly good point on which to comment later.

Why no contemporaneous note? Another discomfort?

Q   You interviewed Sykes in a cell or a room?
A   Detention room, sir.
Q   Was there a table there?
A   Yes, sir.
Q   Chairs?
A   Yes, sir.
Q   Mr Sykes was sitting or standing while being questioned?
A   Sitting, sir.
Q   Were you sitting or standing yourself?
A   Sitting.
Q   Anyone else in the room with you apart from Mr Sykes?
A   D/S Idle, sir.
Q   It seems that you asked all the questions, correct?
A   That's right, sir.
Q   What was D/S Idle doing, just sitting there listening?
A   Yes, sir.
Q   Have you ever heard of a contemporaneous note, officer?
A   Yes, sir.
Q   Was there some reason why D/S Idle could not have taken one?
A   . . .

At this point you may get all manner of answers, all of them helpful to you. It would have been much more 'comfortable' if there *had* been a contemporaneous note, signed at the bottom of each page by the suspect as being correct, and initialled at the end of every line. It is certainly not conclusive of the truth of the interview but it is infinitely more 'comfortable' than evidence written up by the two policemen at some later stage with no opportunity being given to the suspect to sign the record.

Resist the temptation to engage in an argument with the witness as to why he chose not to take a contemporaneous note. Let that come out in re-examination if your opponent dares to deal with it. Leave the matter with a question such as: 'Was there anything which actually prevented you or D/S Idle from being able to make a contemporaneous record?' The answer has to be 'No'. Both the policemen can write. There is paper in the police station. Do not go on. Leave it there. Comment on this 'discomfort' at the end of the trial.

In exactly the same way you can examine all the other 'discomforts' in the evidence. Notice that you are simply asking questions. You are making no comments. You are advancing no criticisms. Yet as you go along you are making your points and you can be sure that they will not be lost on the jury.

And imagine the effect of such questions when they are asked in a quite gentle, inquiring manner, completely without hostility. The jury will be asking for themselves, will be thinking to themselves, the question you yourself will *avoid* asking: 'Why not?' As you examine the discomforts, one by one, they will either be satisfactorily explained or they will not be. If they are not, you are not only building up your armoury of comment for the end. Each failure by the witness to explain a 'discomfort' is its own comment and the jury will not fail to notice.

The simple illustrations given here should have demonstrated another rule which is sometimes described as '*pinning out the victim*'. What it means is that you should get the witness to commit himself on detail before you come to your real point. Take the contemporaneous note issue, earlier. We established that there were table and chairs in the room when the interview took place. We also established that there was another detective in the room who had nothing better to do. All this was established before the question, 'Was there some reason why D/S Idle could nòt have taken a contemporaneous note?' The witness, if inclined to perjury, could not, by this time, explain the note's absence by complaining he had no chair, no table, no assistant.

Establishing the background facts before coming in with the 'punch line' question is vitally important. Get the witness to commit himself in advance. Give him the chance to change the details if he wants to. Be fair. Push him into nothing. But get down to the facts. Pin him down by getting *him* to pin himself down. Otherwise, especially with the experienced witness, he may well slip through your fingers. There is no magic in this. All it requires is that you should know what your objectives are with a particular witness, that you should think clearly and that you should ask yourself at all times, 'What do I need to establish and what is the sensible order in which to do it?'

While the 'discomforts rule', as I have described it, ought to lead you to the weak points of the evidence, and while eliminating possible explanations ought to give you a good store of things to comment on, this, as has been emphasised, is only one way of discrediting the evidence. There are lots of ways of approaching the problem of cross-examination. This is merely a thing to get you started.

Another, and rather obvious, way of discrediting evidence, if you are lucky enough to have the ammunition, is to use a witness's prior *inconsistent statement.* It is astonishing how often witnesses say one thing in a witness statement, accident report, insurance claim, etc., and something quite different in the witness box. Handle such a situation with care. Pin the witness down to what he is saying in the witness box. Get him to testify that he is sure that what he is saying now is correct. Give him all the rope he needs but don't push him. Ask him gently, offhandedly, if he is sure. Does he want to change anything?

Then ask the judge if the witness may see his previous statement. Get him to identify the signature as his. Ask him to read the date. Ask him if he signed it on that date. Ask him the details of how he came to make the statement. Then refer him to the particular lines or paragraphs that are inconsistent with what he is now saying and get *him* to read them out. If he is poor at reading aloud, ask him to follow and to check while you read it out. Ask him regularly if that is what his statement said. If he replies with a 'Yes, but. . .' tell him that you will come back to his explanations in a moment but that you just want first to establish what his statement contains. Get out the bits that you want. Then do what you promised. Go back to the place when he said 'Yes, but. . .'and ask him what he wanted to say. Usually it is a feeble excuse and not an adequate explanation at all that he wants to give you. Let him give it. He is discrediting himself. Deal with the matter in sections if you have a lot of inconsistencies, permitting him to explain his 'Yes, buts . . .' at the end of each section.

Then apply the 'discomforts rule' again. Find those bits that need explanation and put possible explanations to the witness. Was he suffering from some condition on the day when he made his statement that might have befuddled his understanding? Was he coerced, was he frightened, was he rushed? Eliminate them if they can be eliminated. A simple illustration:

Q Forgive me, Mr X, but on (date of statement) were you quite fit and well?

A Yes.

Q I'm not in any sense seeking to pry into your personal affairs, but you were not upset for some reason on that day, were you?

A No, not at all.

Q And — again forgive me — you hadn't been drinking heavily?

A Certainly not.

Q I mean, on the day when you signed that statement you were in good physical and mental health and completely sober?

A Yes.

Q Today you told us (such and such)?

A Yes.

Q Yet in your statement you say something quite different. That is so isn't it?

A Yes.

Q Since making that statement you have, I suppose, talked to people about this case?

A Well . . . uh.

Q Please understand, I'm not criticising that at all. But you have talked to people about this case?

A Well, yes.

Q Can you remember now who those people were . . . ?

Notice that we have *not* asked, 'Why is your testimony different from your statement?' We are keeping a perfectly fair, tight rein on the witness. If the re-examiner wants to — if he can, indeed — sort matters out by asking such a wide and dangerous question, leave it to him. Be kind. Remain kind. Don't embarrass the witness by rubbing his nose in it. It's unpleasant enough for him already. Only if you are opposing a tough professional witness who is refusing to conform to the question-answer requirements should you get tough yourself. Very occasionally you may risk the question, and a double question-comment at that: 'Inconsistent isn't it? Why?' But do take care with such a question. Be sure before you ask it that the witness has already begun to discredit himself. If he has then your risk may be justified and he may lose all credibility by what he says in answer to your rather risky question.

A point which I add here at the suggestion of one of my pupils is this. Whether you choose to cross-examine a witness on his prior inconsistent statement, it is a matter for the judge's discretion as to whether or not that statement should become an exhibit in the case. Two matters, therefore. First, before using the prior inconsistent statement, think carefully about whether it will do your case more harm than good if your opponent successfully applies to have it made an exhibit. If it *is* exhibited then the jury will be entitled to take it with them into the jury room when considering their verdict, and re-reading it as they might, that statement could assume an importance greater than the oral evidence that they heard during the trial. Second, if you decide that it is to your advantage that the jury *should* have the statement in front of them when deliberating on their verdict, then do not forget to apply to the judge for the statement to be exhibited and given an exhibit number. Some time ago we saw our jury come back and ask for a statement that had been cross-examined on to good effect by one of our co-defenders. But he had forgotten to exhibit it and the judge had to refuse the jury's request. It's a point worth thinking about.

Apart from a caution about 'opening the door' (which will be considered under the heading of re-examination) only two further matters need be dealt with. This is, after all, a book of hints for the beginner. Let us have a look at a last useful aid in cross-examination and then consider the way in which to approach the expert witness.

The wedge

First, the useful aid. It might be described as '*driving the wedge*'. Remember your objectives. What are you aiming to do? If, as is usually the case, you are seeking to discredit the evidence, to undermine its worth and reliabilty, then the wedge is a useful tool. You have two or more witnesses giving evidence about the same incident. If you can get one to say one thing and the other to say something different you have driven a wedge between them and both become less reliable.

Remember that witnesses expect to testify about particular things. They have come to court with the salient facts fixed in their minds — and this applies both to witnesses who have come with the intention of telling the truth and to those who have come intending to perjure themselves. They expect to be asked about the central facts: they are far less prepared or able to answer questions about the surrounding details.

The wedge part of your cross-examination ought therefore to begin at the edges, probing the witness's recollection on things which are anything but central to the case. Ask about the weather, the coldness or otherwise of the day, the clothing that people were wearing, the colours of things. Envisage the picture that has been described in chief. Look at the background of that picture: focus your imagination and try yourself to see the detail in it. Then, going around that background in your mind, ask the witness about those details. As his answers come you will modify the image that you have created for yourself, learning more about the scene. You will usually get a lot of 'Don't knows' and 'Can't remembers' but you will get detail as well. (If you don't, and if the witness gives you a 'Can't remember' to all your detail questions then he discredits himself without the need for any wedge.) Pause as you go, and jot down in the shortest note the detail that you get.

When you have exhausted this aspect of the cross-examination turn to other things such as putting your case, making your challenges, laying your ground and so on. But when you come to the next witness ask him about the same detail. If you do it with care you will be surprised how often you get the reward of inconsistency between witnesses. With half a dozen police witnesses the wedge can sometimes prove very useful indeed. When you get an inconsistency, suggest that the witness is wrong. Do it very briefly. 'That's not correct, is it?' 'Yes, it is.' Move on. You have your material on which you can later comment.

Sometimes the wedge is the only approach open to you. It can be awfully tiring to use and it requires a clear head and a good memory. Practise it.

The expert witness

Lastly, a note on the expert witness. In 1982 one of England's leading silks was retained for an enormous case. It was said that the client insisted that for no less than nine months before the date of trial the silk should give up all other work and devote himself entirely to the necessary scientific study that enabled him to handle any expert the other side chose to call. Rumour has it that by the date of trial the silk in question was up to doctorate standard on the particular corner of science that the case turned on.

That doesn't often happen and it isn't likely to happen to you early on. What you will find, however, is that in a case where technicalities are going to be important, you can almost certainly be provided with the assistance of an expert for as many conferences as you need to master the subject. If you use those conferences intelligently you ought to find — perhaps to your surprise — that you quickly come to understand the technicalities more than adequately. Remember two things. First, you are only being required to deal with one narrow aspect of someone else's expertise. Secondly, most experts are a bit shocked to find that other people know anything at all about their subject. Was it Dr Johnson who made a remark about a dog walking on its hind legs? It is not done well but one is surprised to see it done at all. It is in this latter point that the expert's weakness lies. The expert simply is not accustomed to encountering an advocate who actually appears to understand the subject. If you can demonstrate, very early on, that you certainly *do* know something about the subject the expert will become — and this is true of over ninety per cent of them — extremely wary of you. And being wary, not knowing, after all, how much you actually know, he is going to treat you with respect. He is going to be less likely to be dogmatic. He will be more inclined to hedge his bets. He will soften slightly and become more tentative.

Don't forget this: if there is an expert in the case then, as often as not, there will be a dispute arising out of the area of his expertise. This means that in all likelihood there will be at least two views that could be taken on the technical aspect of the case. Any intelligent expert will be aware of this and will be aware that it is his *opinion* of the technicalities that he is being asked about.

He may have come, on the other hand, to a very firm conclusion. In either case the advocate who has done his homework is in with a chance, for if you can get the expert's wary respect early on then the one with the tentative opinion is likely to admit that it is only tentative: he is likely to go along with the alternatives which you suggest to him as being, certainly, possible views which might indeed be correct. If you have an expert with a very firm conclusion then in many cases your apparent expertise is likely to unsettle him a little and he may well start wondering if he is as certain as he thought he was.

These are general observations but one sees them in operation all the time. The rule might be stated thus: *the wary expert is more likely to shift his position.* (If you want to know how the wary expert feels, wait until the first time you encounter a client who actually knows something about the law! We lawyers tend to deal with people to whom the law is an utter mystery. We could tell them that High Trees was a contract dispute about landscape gardening and they would be totally ignorant of our mistake. Doctors are the same. Hundreds of them don't know the difference between progesterone and progestogen but their patients, like our clients, have to take their expertise on trust. But sit across your desk from a lay client who knows the limitations of an Anton Piller order or who can quote sections of the Companies Act at you or who knows which bit of section 22 of the Theft Act has been repealed, and you hear the rustle of the wings of your chickens coming home to roost. 'Well . . . er . . .' you hear yourself saying. The expert in the witness box can quickly be made to feel the same a good deal of the time.)

Let it be said that there are some experts that you can do nothing with. Nothing. If you find that your opponent has called one of the top professors of neurology to talk about his researches into deep pain, then you can know as much as you like about synapses, dendrites, neuro-transmitters *et al* and it will get you nowhere. The witness will be delighted to find you know something about his subject: he is too sure in his honest knowledge to be wary of anyone. In no time at all you will be floored by his profound expertise. What you do then is to back off. If he is so sure he's probably right anyway.

The handwriting expert, oddly enough, is another one that it is incredibly difficult to tackle. He or she usually comes to court with a chart of blown-up photographs which demonstrate with devastating clarity that the two specimens of handwriting were by the same author. It is a case of seeing is believing. If such an expert talks about upward and downward lines and pressure on the paper, seriphs and sweeps and leaves it at that then you are in with a chance. It sounds a bit like scientific mumbo jumbo and it often gets lost on the jury. But if that photographic chart is produced, forget it. All you can do in such circumstances is to comment to the jury that this is trial by jury not trial by expert and remember that you are an advocate, not a magician,

It is the same with the fingerprint expert. If he comes along with a photographic chart and points to the appropriate number of similarities then no matter what you do you are not going to break his evidence. Furthermore he is not going to become wary. The more questions you ask in your attempt to shake him the more you underline the strength of his evidence. If the 'dab' is there then either your client put it there, someone else put it there, or someone is perjuring himself about where it was found. You will not succeed with the expert.

It is as important, in advocacy, to know clearly what *cannot* be done as it is to know what is capable of achievement. So bear in mind that the chart-bearing fingerprint or handwriting expert and the acknowledged leader in his field are all witnesses that it is virtually impossible to crack. All others are capable of being shaken either on the extent of their expertise or on the soundness of their opinion or on their method of investigation. We will glance briefly at these three aspects in turn.

Challenging the extent of the witness's expertise   Nobody — perhaps not even the ultimate leader in the field — knows everything about his subject. If you prepare efficiently and make an in-depth study of just one, tiny area in the witness's expertise, you might well score heavily in the first two minutes. The ultimate example of this concerns the most famous English silk between the wars — Marshall Hall notwithstanding — Norman Birkett. He very rarely prosecuted but, in those days there was a custom (continued into the sixties at least) that when a well-known silk was about to be elevated to the High Court Bench, he was asked, almost as a swan-song to his career at the Bar, to prosecute a notorious murder case. (Swanwick J prosecuted Hanratty, the last man to suffer capital punishment in England, and was appointed almost immediately afterwards.)

Birkett was given the brief to prosecute Rouse, a motorist alleged to have murdered his passenger and then set fire to his car to destroy the body and the evidence. An expert engineer for the defence gave evidence about the fusion of two bits of metal, thereby establishing a powerful point for the accused. Birkett rose to cross-examine.

'What,' he asked in his precise, musical way, 'is the coefficient of expansion of brass?'

And the witness replied, 'I don't know'.

That question had taken him so unawares, had made him so wary of Birkett, that when he was asked: 'You *are* an engineer, aren't you?' the hapless fellow couldn't even get that answer right. He said, 'I suppose so!'

After that all engineering was forgotten. Birkett had destroyed the witness's credibility.

Later, in the Temple, people came up to Birkett and asked him how on earth he had worked out such a devastating first question. He was characteristically modest. 'I simply couldn't think what to ask him', he said. 'It was the first thing that came into my head.'

Parenthetically, that comment raises two matters. First, Birkett's trained instincts as an advocate had led him into asking that expert *anything* which might suggest that Birkett knew a lot about the subject; and we can all dredge up something from our school days on subjects that we abandoned at the age of fifteen. 'What exactly is the crystalline difference between granite and gneiss, doctor?'

Secondly, 'It was the first thing that came into my head' is a much more profound remark than it might at first appear. There are not a few first-rate advocates in practice today who declare that when on their feet in court ideas seem to flow through them. I know one who actively tries to make his mind a total blank for a moment or two before getting up to make a speech. Not many people talk about this but it appears to be a not entirely uncommon attitude of mind. This is not to suggest that such advocates do not prepare as thoroughly as others: that is hardly to be recommended. But many of us — perhaps all — have experienced that thrill of feeling the right words formulate themselves, the right questions asking themselves, the right ideas suddenly slipping into one's awareness. Perhaps, therefore, one of the hints that this handbook should contain is just this: do not be afraid, after you have done your homework, to let your mind slide into neutral just before getting to your feet. There just might be something in it. Certainly it is quietly talked about by a number of very good advocates.

Anyway, back to the expert. No matter what the subject, you ought to be able to find *something* by way of a first question to which the witness might answer 'I don't know'. You, after all, and I, and all of the lawyers in the country just about, could be asked hundreds of such questions. If you can get a 'don't know' from your expert in answer to your first question you achieve two things at once: (a) you make him wary; and (b) you inevitably diminish his credibility with judge and/or jury. If you can get a 'don't know' to your second question, even better. Don't press further. Don't appear unkind. Turn to something else for a moment. Come back for, you hope, some more 'don't knows' later. You will be amazed at how often the expert comes apart. Sometimes he really does not know all that much about his subject and it is difficult then not to batter him around the ring. Do be as kind as you can. If you have to do it, do it regretfully no matter how pleased you may feel with yourself. And keep asking yourself that fundamental question, 'Should I sit down now? Have I got enough?'

Challenging the soundness of the expert's opinion   If it *is* an opinion that the witness is giving then you ought to be armed with the names of the leading works on the subject in question. 'Did you consult (author)?' 'No? Oh! Did you consult (another author)?' 'You didn't? Well, did you consult (third author)?' Then: 'Well, what reference sources did you consult, sir?'

When he gives them ask him the date of publication. Ask if he is aware of any researches that have taken place since then. You should have found out about these things as part of your preparation for the case: you do not embark on such a cross-examination without knowing that such researches have been done, because that would be dishonest. But you can see from this short indication how vulnerable any expert witness can be to the prepared approach. Again, think how vulnerable you as a lawyer would be to such questioning. And it is totally fair.

You must also know exactly what *your* expert witness, if you have one, is going to say, and on what facts he is basing *his* opinion. And as part of 'putting your case', you ought to ask the expert how he deals with your own expert's views. You should be able to end up by getting the adverse expert witness to agree that it is only his opinion that he is giving and that, whatever his views, it is essentially a matter of opinion.

Challenging the expert's method   This is often the only approach when dealing with analysts. The breathalyser laws threw up an enormous cloud of confusion as to what was and was not proper analysis and a lot of people were acquitted because of doubt being thrown on the methods of acquiring the sample, keeping track of it at all times, measuring the quantity being tested and on the methods of the testing itself. If you have made yourself expert for the day in the one narrow field that concerns you, part of your cross-examination can be a step-by-step analysis of how the expert witness went about his task.

'What did you do then?'

'What measurements did you take?'

Already wary, the expert not infrequently finds it unnerving to be taken through his investigations little by little, and since you have boned up on something of the expertise, you might be able to find all manner of small things that were left undone when they should have been done. If you approach it this way you should be able to spot the point at which the expert arrived at his opinion. You may even be able to show that the opinion was premature or that it had been formed upon inadequate methods of fact-finding.

Don't forget that you are entitled to have your own expert sitting in court behind you, available to advise you on the accuracy or otherwise of what the opposing expert is saying. Make sure, however, that you have clearly 'briefed' your expert not to keep barging in, tugging your gown, with unnecessary advice. Get him to make brief notes and pass them silently forward, leaving it to you to decide when you need his more extended guidance.

The important thing is not to be afraid. Do your homework, swot up on the very narrow expertise that you need, know the bibliography that the expert ought to know and, if you have one, understand completely your own expert's report. Cross-examining the expert is not the impossible task it might seem. If you prepare properly and apply all the other principles discussed so far you might well find that it is one of the most enjoyable of all the kinds of cross-examination.

Fifteen

Re-examination

Even more so than with cross-examination, you must ask yourself here, 'Do I need to?' If you can possibly avoid re-examining, then avoid it. Nothing more contemptuously writes off your opponent's efforts at cross-examination than your getting briskly to your feet with the words, 'Unless Your Lordship has any questions?' 'No, Mr Snooks.' 'Then may Mr Sykes return to the dock?' 'Certainly.'

Unless there is some real advantage to be gained or some real point to be made, resist re-examining altogether. If you get up, stand there and pick through your papers, asking two or three feeble or apparently unimportant questions — and one sees it done all the time — you visibly lose your impetus, your authority and your status. You must, when your witness has finished being cross-examined, repossess yourself at once of the running of the show. You must be business-like about it and quietly brisk. Hence, if you do have matters to clear up, you should conduct your re-examination with the utmost economy and the utmost confidence. It cannot be repeated too often: don't re-examine at all if you can safely avoid it. If you must, then be brisk and swift.

During your opponent's cross-examination you should have been scribbling hard, getting down as much as you possibly could of the questions as well as of the answers. In chapter 9 we examined the ideal layout of your notebook, and discussed the need for a two-inch margin on the right of the page. As you note down the cross-examination of your witnesses, into that margin you can put the note 'ReX' whenever something is said which you feel *may* call for re-examination. This enables you to see at a glance those points on which you *might* want to re-examine. Bear in mind that there is no time-lag between the end of cross-examination and your standing up. You have got to be able to react fast, and a clearly flagged trail of possible points is vital at this moment.

There are always lulls in cross-examination. Your opponent may be searching through his papers or taking time to formulate his questions: the judge may be laboriously writing things down. You will have time, here and there, to glance back at the 'ReX' flags in the margin and re-assess them. Make a habit of doing this. If, on reflection, you feel that you can safely leave the point then cross out your 'ReX'. Scrub it through so as to make quite clear that it is eliminated.

During those lulls you ought also to be formulating the way in which to deal with the matters that you decide *do* call for re-examination. You might even jot down the very words that you intend to use in your questions. You should also find time to check back in your notes (if they have been properly kept) to find whether the questions that your opponent has been asking accurately reflect the state of the earlier evidence. You will, in fact, while your opponent is cross-examining, be working flat out — harder than at any other time during the trial. But remember the basic rules about maintaining your status and riding the bumps. Even if you are working nineteen to the dozen, maintain an appearance of cool, ride the bumps without so much as a flicker of distress on your face and radiate a mood of calm. It can be done.

Re-examination was described earlier in this book as a much neglected but potentially sinister art-form. It is just that. The advocates who know how to take advantage of it are comparatively few and all too many find it too tiring and difficult an exercise to engage in more than half-heartedly. It does, after all, require energy and fast thinking.

So do get into the habit of making the necessary gear change and engaging in the somewhat frenetic activity outlined above. If you do, you may succeed in keying yourself up to a sufficient pitch of concentration to be able to use your re-examination to real advantage — always remembering, nevertheless, that no re-examination at all is preferable to anything other than an excellent one.

Bear two other things in mind before we turn to the objects of re-examination. You are back with your own witness now and that means that you are not permitted to ask leading questions except to elicit denials or to recapitulate. The incompetent re-examiner often forgets this. Don't do it yourself and if your opponent does it don't let him get away with it. Despite what has been said earlier about keeping your objections to a minimum this is perhaps an obligatory objection. Just get up and say, 'I do hope my friend is not going to go on leading', and then sit down. The other thing to remember is that you are confined in re-examining to dealing only with those things which 'arose in cross-examination'. This means what it says: you are not entitled to raise new matters that have not been touched on in your opponent's or co-defendants' cross-examination.

Now, why can re-examination be a sinister skill? It is because out of the three objectives of re-examination, two can lead to quite lethal results. The first objective can be stated simply. It is *clarification and clearing up.* Very often your witness has given only half an answer to something and before he had the chance to amplify it he has been swept along by the tide of questioning. If it is of importance, take him back to that answer and get him to explain the whole. For instance:

Q   You were asked by my friend if you were at the Blue Coat Boy on the 3rd of June?
A   Yes.
Q   You said that you were indeed there?
A   Yes.
Q   And he asked you if you had been in the company of (well-known criminal) and (another well-known criminal)?
A   Yes.
Q   And you said that you had?
A   Yes.
Q   He left it at that. I'd like to ask a little more about that day. How long were you at the Blue Coat Boy on that occasion?
A   About ten minutes.
Q   Did you actually have any conversation with (the well-known criminals)?
A   No.
Q   Will you tell us, what were you actually doing in that public house on that occasion?
A   Collecting for the Salvation Army and selling the magazine *WarCry.*
Q   Did you get a contribution from either of the men you were questioned about?

A   No. I rattled my tin at them but they didn't give anything.

An extreme example, no doubt, but it illustrates the point clearly. There is often another half to a picture which utterly alters the whole, and if your opponent has elicited only the half it is sometimes necessary to change everything by filling in the missing bit. Examples of such half-pictures abound in cross-examinations. Add in the missing bits only if by doing so you add a relevant feature to the case or make your opponent look a little silly.

The second objective might irreverently be thought of as *crucifixion*. Rarely is it possible, but the really well prepared advocate just might have the good fortune to have an ace in his hand. Go back to the sergeant on the bicycle, and imagine that the fatal final question had not been asked. The cross-examination would then have ended with the picture of our twenty-stone, hobnailed policeman claiming to have approached in utter silence and the evidence just could not be believed. The re-examining advocate stands up.

Q   You told us both in your evidence in chief and in cross-examination that you approached to within twelve feet of these men and they did not appear to notice your arrival. Is that correct?
A   Yes, sir.
Q   *Did* you get that close to them?
A   Did indeed, sir.
Q   Did they look up?
A   No, sir.
Q   Later, did you have the opportunity of assessing whether they were of normal hearing?
A   Oh, they could hear all right, sir.
Q   Well solve the mystery for us, sergeant. How did you do it?
A   I was on my bicycle, sir.
Q   Yes, thank you, sergeant. May this witness be released, Ma'am? That is the case for the prosecution.

You will not often find yourself with such a card to play, but if ever you do, play it properly.

The third objective of re-examination is to *take advantage of the open door*. This needs to be explained, and it is most easily understood in a criminal context. There are many kinds of evidence that responsible prosecuting counsel will not introduce during his evidence in chief. One simple illustration which will be obvious to everybody is that the prosecution do not adduce evidence about the defendant's previous convictions. (There are minor exceptions to this, as for instance when a person is accused of being in possession of a firearm within five years of being released from prison. Evidence has to be called to the effect that the accused *had* been in prison. But such technical offences are truly exceptions that probe the rule.) Another illustration of evidence which responsible prosecuting advocates will not lead is the statement of somebody who is not before the court and who is not going to be called as a witness. There are many other examples.

Such evidence is not admissible in examination in chief; and if the cross-examiner knows what he is about, the evidence never will become admissible. What so often happens, however, is that by injudicious or plain ignorant questions in cross-examination, the defending advocate lets in evidence that would otherwise be quite excluded. It is said that he 'opens the door' to re-examination: 'kicking open the door' is a better way of describing it because it is usually done unintentionally and through sheer brute carelessness.

If you ask a question about an otherwise inadmissible conversation then you give your opponent the right to examine on the whole of that conversation. If you cross-examine on a document then the whole of that document becomes available as a subject for re-examination. If you introduce character, then character at large is a topic which can be extensively re-examined upon. While many prosecuting advocates do not take advantage of the opened door, there are some who use their opportunities with deadly effect. And this really is the third function of re-examination. It ought to be understood better than it is and it ought to be used more frequently. If it were more widely practised, defending advocates would quickly cotton on and learn to be a bit more circumspect in their cross-examinations.

In one instance the door is often opened not out of stupidity but necessity. If a defendant is going to have to accuse the prosecution witnesses of lying then he is *ipso facto* going to have to attack their characters. With leave of the judge, questions may then be put to the accused concerning his previous convictions and as to *his* character generally. Already in this book it has been recommended that where you know that your character is likely to have to go in, then put it in yourself, bravely, and at the earliest opportunity. But once in, your client's character opens the door to evidence about the character of every witness whom he has attacked. And this is where some experienced advocates use their re-examination to powerful effect.

The defendant has put his character in by questions asked of, say, a police officer. In re-examination the prosecutor may elicit as much detail as he likes about the accused's character. He can go through the whole list of previous convictions and get out the gory details of every one of them. Don't forget that the prosecutor has access to the police files, and the details lurking there are often different from (and far worse than) those which the defendant has recalled and told his lawyers about. More than that, the re-examiner can lead evidence about the character of his attacked witnesses. An illustration — after full details of the defendant's character have been put under the microscope, the re-examiner continues:

Q   Well, now we know something about the man who accuses you of perjuring yourself, officer. May we now know a little about the man whom he accuses? What is your present rank?

A   Detective chief inspector, sir.
Q   How long is it, now, since you became a police officer?
A   Eighteen years, sir.
Q   And how long have you been in the CID?
A   It's twelve years now, sir.
Q   And how long have you held your present rank?
A   Four years, sir.
Q   During your career have you received any commendations from Her Majesty's judges in respect of the performance of your duties?
A   Yes, sir.
Q   Once or more than once?
A   More than once, sir.
Q   How many times, Inspector?
A   Fourteen times, sir.
Q   Yes, I see, fourteen commendations. Have you received any decorations while in the police force?
A   Yes, sir.
Q   Would you be kind enough to give us details? . . .

And so it continues. That can be done with every witness who has been accused of lying, and properly done it can sometimes nail the lid down on the defence. At very least it lets the witness out of the box in a cloud of roses instead of dispatching him with accusations of perjury ringing in everyone's ears.

As you sit there, therefore, scanning your 'ReX' flags in your note-book, ask yourself whether your cross-examining opponent has been kicking open any doors that might provide you with a useful point of entry. If you have mastered the facts of your case you ought to know exactly what evidence you would like to get in, and throughout the cross-examination you should be waiting eagerly for the mistakes that give you your chance. It is this aspect of re-examination that you should work at most assiduously, because not only will its practice make you more effective with your own witnesses, but knowing how to do it yourself will make you more aware of the dangers of cross-examination and your standards will go up all round.

Just one, last cautionary note about re-examination. Remember the rule about expecting no help from your own witness, and remember that, after being cross-examined, your witness will be in a different state of mind from that in which you had him in chief. He will be tired, as like as not, and he may well be truculent. He no longer regards advocates as the friendly fellows that you, in chief, made him feel you were. For this reason take even greater care with him and for this reason ask yourself even more severely whether you actually need to re-examine. It is well worth a final repetition: if you don't do it really well, it's better not to do it at all.

PART THREE

TRIALS WITHOUT A JURY

Sixteen

Advocacy before the professional courts

Introduction

Everything that has been said so far has been based in the main on the kind of advocacy that is appropriate to jury trial. Certainly there have been illustrations here and there of magistrates' courts proceedings, but the thrust of the book has been directed towards jury advocacy. This has been so for the very good reason that the majority of trials that the criminal advocate, anyway, is going to be involved in will be trial by jury. Furthermore, as has already been emphasised, the common law grew up with the jury. The development of our rules of evidence was inherently bound up with that which should and should not be put before a jury; and all the great advocates of the past learned and developed their skills in front of jurors. It is, and probably will always remain, the pivot of British, American and Commonwealth advocacy. If you know the trade of conducting a jury trial then you can modify accordingly for all other tribunals.

This is what we now turn to, and although this section of the handbook is somewhat slender in comparison with what has gone before it is nevertheless as important as any part of the rest. If you make the mistake of approaching the Court of Appeal in the same way as you approach judge and jury you will not survive past your first half minute. The same is usually true for the judge in chambers and for the stipendiary magistrate. All the basic principles discussed so far hold good, but your approach must be substantially modified.

There are many differences between jury and other advocacy but perhaps the fundamental distinction that, if clearly borne in mind, is likely to provide you with the best guidance is this. In trial by jury you are speaking at the same time to two very different creatures — the judge on the one hand and the composite 'animal' of the jury on the other. In a happily conducted trial there are likely to be few conflicts, but if conflict does occur between judge and advocate, the advocate can, and sometimes must, appeal beyond the judge to the jury. In some cases and before some of the more notorious judges it is from the outset a question of fending off the interference of the judge while seeking to reach and hold on to the twelve men and women upon whose collective judgment the outcome depends. In jury trial the judge *can* be overridden. In a justly conducted case there is no need even to think of such a thing: but not all cases *are* justly conducted, and being able to reach past the biased judge is often the name of the game.

Very different it is when you are facing judge alone, or stipendiary magistrate. Nor can you sensibly proceed on the hope of splitting the lay bench, the Court of Appeal or the House of Lords. Justices, Lords Justices and Lords of Appeal in Ordinary may be multiple person courts but they tend to act with ferocious unanimity. Certainly there are disagreements between members of the lay bench, dissenting judgments in the Court of Appeal and differing opinions in the Lords. But the young advocate who felt that there was any change to be got out of playing one part of the court off against the other, would, except in an infinitesimally small number of cases, be deluded to the point of professional insanity. In everything but trial by jury you are stuck with the members of your tribunal. Either you win them or you lose. There is virtually no dividing the field.

From the beginning of a jury trial you are aiming to win the ear and the sympathy of the jury. If you can get that of the judge as well, so much the better, but your prime objective is the jury. In all other courts you are seeking the ear, the sympathy and ultimately the agreement of a very different kind of tribunal and an extra dimension is needed in your advocacy.

The lay and the professional courts

The courts where there is no jury divide into two different kinds, those where the 'judges' are professionally qualified lawyers and those where the bench is made up wholly or in part of people who have no legal qualifications at all. This latter category of courts is composed almost entirely of (a) the magistrates' courts, and (b) the various statutory tribunals. It also includes, of course, the courts martial of the armed services. This division, from the advocate's point of view is fundamental. The approach which is proper when addressing laypeople or a combination of lawyers and laypeople is totally different from the correct approach when appearing before one or more qualified and experienced lawyers.

In all probability your earliest experiences will be in the magistrates' courts, and in the vast majority of the six hundred or so such courts that are scattered throughout England and Wales there sit the lay justices of the peace, assisted or dominated by their clerk. Even the clerk does not have to be a fully qualified lawyer provided he or she has a required amount of legal training, so the possibility is that before the justices you may well find that your advocacy is directed at no lawyers at all.

We will come back to these courts, however, later in the book. Let us look first at the problems which arise out of advocacy in the courts where only the fully qualified lawyers sit.

The professional courts

The clue is to remember the self-evident fact that you are talking to another lawyer. So many young advocates seem not to be aware of this, and it is this lack of awareness which causes most of their mistakes. But just pause and think for a moment. If you have got to the point when you are cutting your teeth in advocacy you must surely have acquired some liking for the law. I suppose it must be possible, but I certainly don't think it very common to find on the bench a professional lawyer who doesn't rather enjoy the law. Some of them absolutely love it. Lord Edmund-Davies, when leaving the Court of Appeal for the House of Lords, talked of how lucky he had always felt actually to be paid for doing something he enjoyed so much. Don't forget that among those who like the law there exists a kind of fraternity. Don't forget either that even Lords of Appeal in Ordinary were once young advocates, faced with the same kind of problems as face you today. And lastly, don't forget that in thirty years from now it is you or your contemporaries who will be sitting as our judges and

Lords Justices. Without yielding in the slightest to sentimentality, permit yourself to be aware that the law is made up of overlapping generations. Try to temper in yourself the feeling that *he* is a judge and *you* are an advocate. The truth is that you are both lawyers, your careers may have much in common and it may be that only the time-scale is substantially different.

Imagine yourself back in a particularly good tutorial or supervision, discussing an interesting point of law with a good law teacher. There was probably formality between you but the nature of your communication was discussion, conversation. If your law-don asked you a question you would not have harangued him with some long oratorical answer stitched up with repetitions and nervousness. You would have done your best to answer him simply, directly and accurately. You would have repeated yourself only to make a particularly emphatic point and you would have acknowledged that you were repeating yourself for that reason. You would have taken no more time about your answer than was necessary. You both knew, after all, that you had other things to move on to. What is more, you would not have insulted your law-don's intelligence by telling him elementary things that he might be expected to know. If you did feel it necessary to refer to something which you both knew, you would have — as it were — apologised for so doing and would have explained why it seemed proper for you to do it.

If you approach the lawyers on the bench in the same spirit as you encountered your notional law-don, you will to some extent automatically avoid many mistakes. It is difficult to make a speech at someone if you feel, rather, that you are in conversation with him, and making a speech at your professional court is a terrible mistake. Likewise, if you are in conversation, or feel that you are in conversation, you are unlikely to repeat yourself without apology. Again, if you school yourself into feeling conversational you simply will not engage in that ghastly left-over sometimes called the peroration, which, with a professional court goes down like the proverbial lead balloon.

Note that the advice is to *feel* conversational. You have to maintain formality. You dare not become chatty and your language must remain courteous and correct. But if you cultivate that feeling you will be going in the right direction.

Some basic rules

Now, we are about to look at some basic rules that should help you face the professional court. They may seem a bit intimidating, and for this reason it seems a good idea to tell you in advance how best to put them into effect. Experience is something you cannot get out of a book and experience is the biggest help of all, particularly with the professional court. You have to make up for this, therefore, by sheer hard work.

You simply must be well prepared. You must know your facts and you must know your law and you must be able to find your way around your papers and your authorities with all the nimble speed at your command. In cases where you have bundles of documents, make sure that they are paginated and if necessary flagged. You can get at most stationers a 'butterfly brand' indexing strip which can be cut to convenient lengths and marked. You may find this an invaluable aid in locating documents. You can also get folders of the kind that have a heavy spring running the length of their spine such that you can turn a bundle of papers an inch thick into the equivalent of a bound volume in the twinkling of an eye. Consider making a habit of photocopying your authorities and carrying them, suitably flagged in such folders. The photocopied law report has the advantage of being wondrously transportable with the even greater advantage that you can underline it, make notes in the margin and so on.

Get your papers into apple-pie order and know them completely. Check on all the up-to-date supplements to see that you have the law at your fingertips. Read the regular publications religiously and go to the textbooks and even to your own college notes to check up on the subject of your case. If you go to court to ask a judge to make an order of any kind, know what authority he has for making that order and be ready to quote it, chapter and verse. You are your client's lawyer. Do these things. If you were his anaesthetist you would take such meticulous preparation utterly for granted. Yet so many lawyers feel that such an approach derogates from the dear old amateurism of the advocate. If you do take your preparation really seriously you will start with a huge advantage in the professional court because preparation shows, just as lack of preparation shows. And our judges and stipendiary magistrates have become so accustomed to second-rate preparation by advocates that they will be pleasantly surprised when they see — as they most certainly will — that you have taken your job seriously.

Remember again what was said about the fact that we are all lawyers. One cannot fail to feel respect for the lawyer who has clearly got his case properly prepared. Even if he is stumbling through his first appearance the professional court will see that effort has gone into his preparation and he will be given full marks for that. And as we know from a long way back in this book, getting and keeping the sympathy of the court is vital. By truly thorough preparation you will begin to attract that sympathy. You will also be far better able to put into effect the rules that follow. Apart from any other reason, there is nothing else you can do at first.

Now, these rules.

Economy in everything is your byword.   This means in your speech, in the language you choose, in the time you take to find the right document, in your pace. In everything about you, you should seek to convey that you don't want to take a moment longer than is necessary. Do not overdo it to the point where you appear rushed or agitated. That would be self-defeating. Cool, controlled economy is what you are seeking to convey. You must get the message across that you are vitally aware that time is running. If you manage this, it will do you more good than just about anything else.

Do not repeat yourself without acknowledging that you are doing so. With a jury a certain amount of repetition is essential. Some excellent speeches are constructed like a rondo with a theme song being returned to at intervals. Don't do it with a professional court. If you regard your judge as a lawyer, and an experienced one at that, you should see why it is an insult to his intelligence if you make the same point twice. If you use repetition, do so only in order to emphasise the most important points and acknowledge that you know what you are doing. 'Sir, it really does deserve to be emphasised and you'll forgive me if I repeat myself very briefly but . . .. '

Never underestimate the intelligence of your professional court. The arrogance of the young is astonishing. To be fair, however, you wouldn't be trying your hand at advocacy unless there was a touch of arrogance or something like it in your character. But control it. Unless and until it is quite clear to you that you are before one of the few really silly lawyers who have somehow been appointed to sit in judgment on the rest of us, do please assume that your judge is at least as clever as you are. This way you will avoid some terrible mistakes.

I remember once appearing in quarter sessions in the little town of Devizes. It had taken one scheduled and one unscheduled train journey followed by a horribly expensive taxi ride to get there, and for all the good it did my client I might as well have stayed in bed. Ahead of me in the list was a splendid young barrister who delivered to the chairman of the bench a beautiful and condescending lecture on the elementary principles of sentencing. He sat there in his rusty tweeds, did the chairman, looking something between bemused and bored. He said nothing as our hero went blithely on, but when the time came he didn't accede to his eloquent plea for leniency either. The young man departed the court without ever having discovered that he had just appeared before Lord Devlin, then retired as a Lord of Appeal in Ordinary and filling in a spare day as 'qualified chairman' of the bench.

Do be careful, especially after the frightening newness of everything has worn off. No matter who he may be, the man on the bench had quite a bit of experience before he became a judge and it is a grave mistake to underestimate him.

Be aware that the professional court can talk back. This is another, and at first shocking, difference between this kind of tribunal and the jury. One delightful judge privately confides that if he doesn't talk back then he has stopped listening. He says that when bored he quietly does abdominal exercises on the bench, waiting until something interesting turns up. Oddly enough he is not immediately recognisable for his board-like abdomen, which no doubt indicates that he is not as often bored as he claims to be. This talking back is a bit unnerving at first but once you have got used to it, it is of great value. In this way you find that you get into real conversation with your tribunal and you are thereby enabled to see, at least to some extent, the way its mind is working. This leads on to the next rule.

If your judge accords you the privilege of telling you what he is thinking, do not abuse that privilege. Deal with the matters he has expressed interest in. 'I see exactly what Your Lordship is saying. Can I come straightaway to that?' And deal with it. Be ready to abandon in mid-flight the point that you have been making. Turn at once to deal with the thing in which your tribunal has expressed interest. You can always, if necessary, come back to what you were talking about before you were interrupted. With the professional court you must *never* in your early years say anything remotely like, 'I shall come to that in a moment.' Deal with it there and then. If you don't then you are failing to keep your court happy and you risk losing sympathy. When you want to get back to the (hopefully useful) point that you were making before the judge's interjection, you can either go there without introduction or you can say something like: 'Before Your Honour was kind enough to draw my attention to this matter — which I trust I've now dealt with to Your Honour's satisfaction — I was referring to (put it very shortly). Can I return briefly to that?' He will either say something like, 'By all means, Mr Snooks' or he will indicate something else in which he's interested. Never make him wait. Deal with what he's interested in as soon as he accords you the privilege of indicating what it is.

In the Court of Appeal this is what it is all about. We will come back to this later. Next, and connected with the last two, is the following rule.

Try to engage your tribunal in conversation. Aim to get the judge talking. You can't *make* him do this, but if you *can* get him talking, so much the better. If you both go away feeling that the whole exercise has been a helpful and interesting interchange of ideas between lawyers then the case will not have been lost by your advocacy. You may not win but remember what was said earlier about ninety per cent of cases deciding themselves. There is no technique recommended to get your judge to open up. If you are really well prepared he will probably take over anyway. You can, if you want to, take the bull by the horns and say something like: 'I'm anxious not to weary Your Lordship with unnecessary submissions. I don't know if Your Lordship would find it useful if I developed (such and such a point).' It takes a hard man not to give you an indication there. But feel it out for yourself. As long as you are aware of the concept you are on the right road.

It has already been stated in general terms but it bears repeating as a rule:

Do not make a speech to your professional court. Pause here for a moment and think again. If your client is present (and this can mean your lay client, or, if you are a member of the Bar, your solicitor, referred to as your 'professional client') you may very well be tempted to give them so many inches of transcript in order to make them feel that you've tried your best for them. Don't do it. When you are before a professional court put all ideas of impressing your clients completely out of your mind. You have a job to do: it is to relate to that judge or to those judges who are going to decide your case. It is good tactics to explain this in advance to your clients.

'I may be very boring indeed', you can say. 'And I may not deal with half a dozen points that you think are important. That won't be because I have forgotten them. If I leave them out it will be because I feel that that's the best way of handling it. All right by you?'

You always get the answer 'yes' to such a question and it leaves the client feeling that things are, as they ought to be, completely under control. So many advocates — especially in England, where the solicitor has always stood between barrister and lay client — ignore the humanities of the situation. You need freedom to conduct the trial as you feel it ought to be conducted. You must have that freedom, otherwise you may well mess up the whole thing. So think of your poor client. Tell him in advance that leaving out is as important as including in. If you do, he will trust you. If you don't, you'll risk having an unhappy client no matter what the result. That would be a total failure of the private advocacy that ought to have taken place between client and lawyer.

But having diverted to this important relationship between client and advocate, let's now get back to the rule — don't make a speech at your professional court. Ask if you may summarise your points by all means, then do so as if the taximeter had gone on to double time. But do not weary the professional court with a client-orientated summation. The gratitude that the judge will feel to you will be almost inordinate. I recently heard a neat, simple ending to a long, complicated and very economical submission:

'Those are the matters I put before Your Lordship and I don't think they gain anything by repetition. Unless there is anything specific that Your Lordship would like me to deal with more fully, that's how I put it.'

'No, thank you, Mr Snooks. You have put your submissions with admirable clarity, if I may say so.'

'Your Lordship's most kind.'

It was a mutual stroking exercise and that is what it really ought to be about.

'My Lord, I can be very brief' is a marvellous beginning to final submissions.

'My Lord, I'm afraid that I'm not going to be able to deal with this as shortly as I'd like to' is also good. In accordance with the equal and opposite rule, it evokes the reply, 'Take all the time you need Mr Snooks'.

Both approaches acknowledge that you know the taximeter is running, and it is almost the definitive mark of the good advocate that he recognises and conveys that he recognises the value of time.

Lastly, *sympathise with their lot from beginning to end.* This has been dealt with at some length earlier in the book. Always keep it in mind. If you go to the Court of Appeal and listen to the exhausting, repetitious banalities that the distinguished lawyers sitting there have to put up with, you may find yourself reflecting on what a strange system we work to. What other job in the world can you think of that requires three men of top-rate mental ability to sit in patient silence while listening for hours to ill-judged applications unprofessionally argued by advocates who as often as not have failed to make proper preparation? In the United States the appellate judges are protected by time limits that firmly restrict how much an advocate can say; but in England there is no such protection for the judges. If the professional courts are going to refuse an application then they are usually anxious to let the advocate say all he wants to say. Otherwise, if they cut the lawyer short and then turn him away, unsuccessful, complaint might be made that the loser wasn't given a fair hearing. Make a point of going into the Queen's Bench Divisional Court of a morning or into the Criminal Division of the Court of Appeal when appeals against sentence are being dealt with. Don't think how tetchy the judges are but rather observe the stoic patience that they exhibit.

When you come before any professional court remember this. *You* don't have to sit there for five hours a day exposed to the disorganised oratory of people whom, by definition, you were better than. When you come before the lawyers who left the hurly-burly of advocacy and took the holy water of the bench, respect them. A lot of them wish they could come down and do it for you. In fact, apply the rule that has been repeated again and again in this book: be kind.

Now, with those eight general rules under your belt let us look — and we can do it fairly briefly — at the modifications for the different kinds of professional courts that you will ultimately come before.

The Court of Appeal   Here the taximeter is on triple time. Do not waste a second. Have *everything* at your fingertips. Write out the preliminaries so that you can whip through them with stately immediacy. Tell the court if you can that you are abandoning half your grounds of appeal and concentrating only on this, this, and this. Tell them that your submissions can be briefly stated. If you have a point that cannot be put shortly tell them that you may have to tax their patience for a little while as you develop your submissions on ground (whatever) but you hope that you will do it as shortly as possible. Urgency and economy rule. Go and watch it done. Remember that they are absolutely brilliant lawyers. They will usually grasp points quicker than you thought possible.

Oddly enough, they are not a terrifying court if you are absolutely prepared. They are, with the House of Lords, the most conversational court of the lot. Be prepared to abandon your script almost at once. You are in there to answer questions. More than any other court they are lawyers who enjoy talking to economical lawyers. Infinite respect, perfect preparation, a point worth taking their time over and a clear demonstration that you understand the value of time are all you need. If you have these they will listen, help, question and, indeed, tolerate your inexperience. They are the most unforgiving court in the land to the inadequately prepared and to the time-waster. To the well prepared and the meter watcher they are the nicest tribunal of all — with the possible exception of the Lords.

The High Court Judge. To a *very* slightly lesser extent, apply the same principles as have been set out for the Court of Appeal. Often he or she is much more indulgent but never take advantage of that. In England when a man is appointed to the High Court bench he gets a knighthood: when a woman is appointed she is made a Dame. They are social distinctions of a degree that rightly reflect the professional distinction that they have, almost all of them, justifiably earned. When you meet the judge in chambers, aim to pare down what you have to say to the economical minimum. Brisk accuracy and economy are your objectives. If you are seen to be brief and to the point you are half-way there. If you are utterly prepared as well you are three quarters of the way there.

The Queen's Bench Master, the Family Division Registrar and the District Registrar. Informality is much greater here, but keep it totally formal until you get to know the Master in question. Speed is of the essence here as in the Court of Appeal. Again, remember that he is a lawyer and that his experience is simply vast. He has to suffer fools, day after day. Don't be one of them.

The Chancery Master. One dare say very little about this rare and charming breed. Whenever I have come before them they have seemed utterly delightful, very much less harassed than some of the Queen's Bench Masters and always willing to point a novice gently and encouragingly in the right direction. If you are likely to have dealings before the Chancery Masters consult your pupil master about their individual likes and dislikes. There is no more exclusive club in the world than the English Chancery Bar and no one outside their ranks would hazard any comment save this: if the whole of the English, American, Canadian and Australian Bars, and the rest of the legal profession of the Common Law, knew what they were about with the precision and exactness of the English Chancery Bar, the law as a whole would be a much, much better thing.

The County Court/Circuit Judge. There are over three hundred such judges in England and Wales. They divide their time between Crown Court crime, matrimonial work and the smaller civil disputes. They vary in quality very considerably. Some of them are quite excellent, some of them astonishingly obtuse. For your purposes conduct yourself as you would do before the High Court judge — exactly. The difference in the mode of address you will remember. 'My Lord' or 'My Lady' for the High Court judge; 'Your Honour' for the county court/circuit judge. Remember that when sitting in the county court the judge is exposed to a large number of unrepresented litigants. He not infrequently grants right of audience to solicitors' clerks and, especially in the provinces, the professional advocates who tend to come before him include the newest and least experienced solicitors in his area. He is exposed to a rich variety of advocacy, most of it pretty dreadful. For this reason his patience has been sorely tried over and over again. He may have become either remarkably mild or very bitter in the face of all this. But against this backdrop you will see what an opportunity presents itself to any young advocate who has taken his calling seriously, who has tried to learn the rules and who is really well prepared.

The Stipendiary Magistrate. Although there is often quite considerable informality in the 'Stipe's' court you should adopt the same approach to him as you would to the Court of Appeal. He has to get through an enormous case-load on the days when he sits and he is exposed to the most awful advocacy in the country. He has heard the same story over and over again and has endured the same platitudes being trotted out for him by the succeeding generations. He has tended to become case-hardened and has fought against it. He has an understandable inclination to favour the police and he is usually wise. Your approach should be fast, urgent, economical and respectful. It is to be emphasised: behave as you would towards the Court of Appeal. And don't forget the rule about showing him the way home.

Finally, let us turn, in the last chapter, to a curiously British institution.

Seventeen

Advocacy before the non-professional courts

In most countries judging is done by soldiers or qualified lawyers. In England, however, a truly vast amount of court work is handled by laypeople acting as judges. We will deal here with the three main sorts of non-professional courts, namely the magistrates' courts where the stipendiary does not sit, the statutory tribunals and the courts martial.

Justices of the peace

By way of introduction this much should perhaps be said. A lot of people who are involved with the law run the risk of feeling a bit self-important. Quite a few lawyers do, quite a few judges. Having influence over the liberty and the immediate rights of others is a strange and powerful thing. After all, most people have virtually no power of control over anybody. Far more feel the sensation of helplessness than ever experience the feeling of power.

The layperson who is elevated to sit in judgment on his fellows suddenly acquires an extraordinarily real power. He or she can fine, imprison, silence, remand and order. Collectively these laypeople, sitting to decide on the granting of licences, can bankrupt thriving business concerns and reduce the affluent to financial hardship. They can stamp out careers, split families, attribute paternity. They can issue solemn threats and they can authorise all manner of invasions against the liberty of their fellow citizens. It's power all right, and if the holder of that power occasionally suffers, as lawyers sometimes do, from feelings of self-importance, then perhaps it is not to be wondered at.

Who are these laypeople anyway? What special qualifications do they have? Surprisingly, the answer is virtually none. They used to be members of the old squirearchy, notable citizens, people of substance and influence in the locality. They now come from all walks of life. They include local politicians, trade union officials, retired headmistresses, shopkeepers and businessmen — they are, in fact, a cross-section of the more substantial and 'respectable' people in the neighbourhood. You might and you occasionally do find, out of London, the local Duke chairing the lay bench. Certainly the aristocracy are still well represented among the justices of the peace, and one of the odd experiences of the young advocate is to turn up at some remote magistrates' court to find all the locals addressing the chairman as 'My Lord'. I recall once, many years ago, being in a court where everyone addressed the amiable old boy in the middle as 'Your Grace'. I called him 'Sir'. So will you.

You will find that some lay benches are utterly charming and intelligent. Others you will encounter that are rough, rude and apparently dense. Most come somewhere in between the two extremes. But you simply must remember that in their neighbourhood they are quite powerful people and some of them are, understandably, a bit conscious of it. This realisation should take you right back to the first rule proposed in this book on the principles of advocacy: 'Know your audience and adjust your approach accordingly'. Treat them all with respect. If you are evidently well prepared and know your case and if you follow the rules enunciated so far, they will certainly treat *you* with respect.

It can be a nicely balanced relationship. As responsible people of their neighbourhood they have an instinctive admiration for the fact that you distinguished yourself in your studies and had the pertinacity to carry them through to the point of qualifying as a lawyer. You in your turn ought to have in mind that by being chosen to be the justices of the peace of their neighbourhood they too have distinguished themselves.

Be aware of this potential 'balance of respect', because it is both justified and useful. There is not uncommonly a tendency among some young advocates to think of the lay justices as being a crowd of woodentops, as people who think illogically, who cannot be relied upon to come up with a sensible decision and who, being unqualified, are somehow inferior. That is such a silly mistake.

Of course, the justices can be perverse, and of course their absence of immersion in legal thought sometimes creates a communication gap between bench and lawyer. But if you start to think of them as inferiors you will inevitably talk down to them. That is the flavour that will inform your advocacy. You will never get the sympathy of your court and it will serve you right. Quite apart from anything else, they might, despite their appearance, be better qualified, better educated and cleverer than you. Hidden behind their usually unexceptionable facades you might find all manner of interesting backgrounds.

We can go back, therefore, to an already familiar rule: don't underestimate the intelligence of your tribunal. Always aim to feel that the bench are worthy of your respect and you will thereby avoid the wrong flavour. At the same time you will lay the foundation for that different kind of rapport that can exist. With the professional court you aim to communicate on a lawyer to lawyer basis. With the non-professional court you aim to communicate as different kinds of people both of whom have considerable respect for the accomplishments of the other.

Understand this from the earliest possible moment and you will find that it quite often adds a dimension of niceness to your appearances before the lay bench. You will particularly find, as a young advocate going to a court in the country, that your arrival is often treated with considerable sense of occasion. Everybody from chairman of the bench down to the usher is pleased to have counsel appearing before them and they are concerned to make you feel welcome. Reciprocate their respect for you. It makes the administration of justice so much easier. But let me add a caveat. When the first edition of this book came out I received many letters from magistrates and their clerks. While they agreed with all that had been said they also pointed out that many barristers are incredibly verbose and time-wasting. Solicitors, they said, tended to be more brief and to the point. Whether you are barrister or solicitor, therefore, keep in mind the paramount need for economy in all you do.

Come now to that remarkable English official, the clerk to the justices. Out in the provinces he's often a retired solicitor in late middle age. In the big cities he or she might be a fully qualified barrister or solicitor or a civil servant who is a member of neither profession but who has received extensive legal training in the jurisdiction, practice and procedure of the magistrates' court. The function of the clerk is to advise the lay justices on the law, to run the court and to take depositions.

In the old days everywhere, and nowadays in many places still, you would be forgiven for thinking that the proprietor of the court was the clerk himself. Some of them still dominate their courts to a quite astonishing degree. Comyn J, as a very young junior, doodled a verse on his way back from the West Country once:

> I'm the power beneath the throne:
> I'm the way the wind has blown:
> I'm the man who knows his 'Stone'.
> I'm the Clerk!

Now the right relationship with the clerk is probably more of a hit or miss affair than anything else in advocacy. It is a strange office that he occupies — the lawyer who acts as some kind of major-domo to the unqualified justices, a sort of butler or master of ceremonies to the laymen, a learned adviser but not, in theory at least, a decision taker. He sits, as Comyn J observes, 'beneath the throne'. He decides so much, yet the ultimate decisions aren't his.

In all of this he may be thoroughly happy. He may never have seen himself in wig and gown enthralling an Old Bailey jury. He may hug himself in warm self-congratulation whenever he thinks of his regulated pensionable life. He may on the other hand be as desperate as Jude the Obscure, hating every last moment of his safe existence and resenting bitterly the carefree young advocates who have snapped up chances that he either failed to grasp himself or never had. He may be neither of these. He may just be a grumpy old solicitor who has got tired to death of the job. He may be a tough, stiff-necked, bossy individual who adores the power he exercises. He may be a kind, contented chap who enjoys every minute of his interesting and useful profession.

Which of these he is, you will not and cannot know at first. With clerks whose court you only visit once you may never find out. With courts you go to often the reality will become apparent very soon and you will have to adjust in order to cope with it. With a clerk who is doing his job properly and who is internally adjusted, you ought — ought, mind you — to have little trouble. If you are prepared as you ought to be, with your facts and your law at your fingertips, you will not encounter difficulties. But the clerk is the part of the lay bench court that is in the habit of talking back. Very often he interrupts.

'What is the relevance of that?'

'How can that be right?'

If you are not ready for this and don't know how to cope, the clerk can throw you off balance with ease.

What your attitude ought to be to such intrusions is awfully difficult to advise you about. In some courts the relationship between the lay justices and their clerk is so close, so interproprietorial, that an attempted protest against the clerk will be taken as a personal affront by the bench. In others you can appeal to the chairman: 'Sir, I am seeking to address you. I am seeking to do so as succinctly as possible and I fear that I am being very much hampered by your learned clerk!' And you may get a reassuring 'Yes, do go on, Mr Snooks. We have the point you are making.'

At first you have no choice but to proceed on the basis that the clerk and the justices are the best of friends. Avoid conflict with him if you possibly can. Bear in mind that, as in most other courts, your state of preparation will rapidly become apparent and as a person of considerable legal experience the clerk is likely to have respect for you if you are visibly well prepared. Let him interrupt if he must and only seek to appeal over his head when you feel *sure* that he is being unfair. If you appear regularly in his court you will rapidly find out whether or not his justices will tolerate an appeal against his barracking.

If they will not, then you are landed with the somewhat humiliating task of flattering the fellow. You will have to get to know him, call him by his name, make references to his help when you address the justices, treat him as an 'important person'. Obsequious though you may have to be, it is sometimes the only way of getting anything like justice for your client. Furthermore, if you do succeed in winning the respect of such a clerk you will probably attract the admiring approval of the court officers, the policemen who, one to each court-room, manage the lists and determine in which order the cases are called. The importance of getting on with these people can hardly be over-emphasised from a purely practical point of view.

Advocacy before the lay bench is much less 'high pressure' than before the professional courts but not as free as it can be before a jury. You have a very slightly smaller need than before the professional court to convey that you are striving not to take up any more time than you need. Brevity, control of all you are doing and the like are as much required as ever, but because you are a professional in the presence of laypeople you can permit yourself a very small measure of latitude and can dictate your own pace just a little. The occasional rhetorical question is acceptable, as with a jury, and you *do* dare repeat yourself, but under very tight rein.

Do not dwell long on the burden of proof because they have heard it so very often before. If you feel it essential to spend a little time on it, then apologise for it.

> 'Do forgive me if I seem here to say something that you are already so familiar with, but I want my client to know that this has been said on his behalf and not just understood between us . . ..'

If you indicate to them that you are not proceeding on the foolish assumption that they have never heard before what you are now saying to them they will bear with you in patience. Apply this principle as consistently as you can. Without actually saying as much, approach them on the basis of 'We both know what we are talking about. I know that you know and you know that I know.'

In your final submissions you *can* make a mini-speech. It's a good notion to begin with some such phrases as, 'Ma'am, I shall be very short. I have four points that I'd ask you to consider and I shall try very hard not to repeat myself.' Then get into your points.

Apart from these slight variations of attitude, try to apply all the principles that have already been discussed.

Statutory tribunals

Here you have a legally qualified chairman and, usually, two laymen who are representatives of political or factional interests. The rules are *very* much eased up here. *If what you say sounds like advocacy, then you are doing it wrong.* The atmosphere is much more one of quietly trying to find out the right thing to do.

These tribunals often feel more like a well run committee meeting than a court of law. Fastidious politeness is required, as always, and a great deal of quiet kindness. Non-lawyers often appear as advocates and it will do you a power of good to play down your 'lawyerliness'. The helpful, 'well groomed civil servant' approach is called for. Never a purple passage, please. Never the expansive phrase or gesture. Quiet, totally well organised, efficient and gentle: those words pretty well describe the kind of young advocate who goes down well in the tribunals.

It is a knack that you will develop, the ability to be very slightly self-effacing in these quasi-courts. They hold no terrors at all to the well-prepared. Their members are patient and respectful of competent lawyers. There are no tetchy clerks. Formality is at an absolute minimum. Go along to them determined just to be a well-prepared, nice individual. When you have to discuss law, do so with a measure of reluctance, despite the fact that labour law can be as complex as anything that the Vice-Chancellor might have to deal with. To sum it up in a sentence, avoid appearing to be a lawyer before the statutory tribunals. Go along there as someone whose presence is just going to be of assistance in the important work they have to do.

Courts martial

Very different indeed is the court martial and although this is a tribunal which many young advocates will never encounter, it deserves mention in this book for two reasons. Firstly, a limited number of young advocates most certainly will find themselves instructed to defend before a court martial, and I know of no short publication which will tell them what to expect. Secondly, the young barrister will find that in courts martial there will be no instructing solicitor and he may find it helpful to know what he is entitled to do.

Where does this kind of court fit into the common law system of justice? Expressed briefly the position is as follows. Members of the armed forces (and in certain circumstances their immediate family) are subject to military, air force or naval law. Discipline in the armed forces is maintained by the sanction of minor punishments, imposed by an officer sitting as if he were a kind of stipendiary magistrate, and by major punishments imposed by a court martial. Purely military offences are dealt with by one or other of these methods of disposal, but if a member of the armed forces commits a purely civilian offence he can be and often is brought before a court martial and both tried and punished for it.

There are two kinds. The *general court martial* consists of five serving offices and a judge advocate. It hears serious cases and all cases in which the defendant is of commissioned rank. The *district court martial* consists of three serving officers, usually sitting with a judge advocate, and handles the less serious offences. The judge advocate is a fully qualified and usually quite experienced lawyer who is a full-time, salaried member of the staff of the Judge Advocate-General. His function in the court martial is to act as a cross between a Crown Court judge and clerk to the justices. Both in theory and in practice the final authority of the court is in the president (the senior officer) acting on behalf of the majority of the officer members, but the judge advocate is accorded the right to 'run' the trial as if he were a judge sitting with a jury. He, therefore, tends to be the part of your court who talks back. He makes sure that the rules of evidence are complied with and he, in practice, will decide on objections taken during the hearing. At the end the judge advocate directs the officer members on the applicable law and sums up on fact. He then *withdraws entirely* and the officers deliberate on their verdict much in the same way as a jury or a bench of lay justices. At all other stages in the case, the judge advocate sits as part of the court and contributes to its decisions.

The senior officer in a general court martial is usually a full colonel, captain RN or group captain. In a district court martial the president is a lieutenant-colonel, commander or wing commander. In both kinds the other officers are of assorted descending rank. Much formality is observed. Medals are worn, the judge advocate is robed and wigged (in a wig worn by no other kind of lawyer) and the defending barristers wear wig and gown, solicitors, bands, dark suits and gowns. There is a vast amount of saluting and foot stamping by the non-commissioned ranks and as a visiting defence lawyer you will be treated with enormous courtesy and respect both in and out of the court-room.

You will also be given an astonishingly warm welcome. Everything that can be will be done to make you completely comfortable. Nothing will be too much trouble. Cars will not infrequently be put at your disposal and you will be inclined from time to time to reflect on how different it all is from the dear old Tottenham Magistrates' Court. For court-martialling tends to be the young man's trade. The fees are at best modest and the court-room is usually out of England, so the contrast with your usual magistrates' court is a real one.

Your advocacy should be the same as for the lay justices, though you are entitled to develop the burden of proof with some emphasis. Indeed, do this briefly but as forcefully as you can: the members of a court martial sometimes need reminding that the presumption of innocence applies in the forces as well as in civilian life. Be as 'real' as you can in your advocacy. They expect you to be some kind of 'legal eagle' and will be even more pleased to have you there when they find out that you talk standard English and make easily recognisable sense. Be fastidiously polite. The rule about being as nice as you can is easy to follow in a court martial because everyone else is being so pleasant. But be a bit formal as well. Fit your approach to the occasion.

They are never in a hurry. Unlike any other court they usually have all the time in the world for if they weren't doing this they would be back at their normal duties. For them it is something of a rarity, a novelty even, and as well as taking the whole thing with utmost seriousness they regard serving on a court martial as an interesting experience. So while you must not bore them, you can regard this as the one court where you can let up on the pressure to convey that you are not prodigal with time. In view of your attitude towards the use of time which you should have developed by now, you may even have to slow down a bit lest they feel you are rushing things.

Do remember that they are having the chance of a really close look at a professional lawyer in operation, possibly for the first time. And a point worth remembering is this: in much the same way as you can become expert for the day in a technical dispute in order to be able to cross-examine the adverse expert witness, so these professional officers in the armed forces will usually have attempted to become expert for the day in the little area of law which the trial involves. They will have read it up in the excellent manuals of military, naval or air force law which are published by HMSO. They may well have it at their fingertips and they will not only be bewildered but also disappointed if they find that you are not equally well-prepared. More than that, the members of your court martial may also have been required, at some stage in their careers, to act as a 'soldier's friend', a non-professional defending advocate. So you could well find that some of them will have tried to do themselves what they are now watching you do. For these reasons you must regard yourself as a representative of the entire profession and do your best not to let us all down.

Furthermore, at the lunch-time adjournment you will all go together to the Mess where you will be bought pre-lunch drinks by the members of your court or by your judge advocate! At first it's a very strange sensation, but it does nothing to impede the administration of justice. Nothing, that is, unless you take a wee bit too much and find yourself affected in the afternoon. The most valuable word of warning you can be given on the subject of courts martial is that in Germany the measures of gin begin as doubles. So, remember what was said about being the first lawyer that they have probably had the chance of getting a close look at. Watch your step at the bar where you will undoubtedly be plied with the duty-free, and remember that you are, in these special circumstances, a very real representative of your profession.

Since you are (except on the rarest occasions) the only lawyer for the defence, you are permitted to deal direct with not only your client but all witnesses as well. Indeed you have to find out for yourself, sometimes, if there *are* any witnesses. You will have an officer to help you and if you want to interview someone or have a view, it will all be arranged at the drop of a hat. You can ask for investigations to be made and they will be. If you really have good cause for it an adjournment will be readily granted. Witnesses will be flown out from England, books specially got for you. The services take justice with utmost seriousness and want everything to be done exactly to the letter. You will also get a great deal of help from your opponent who is a qualified barrister or solicitor in service uniform. Anything you need to know he will help you with, especially any technicalities in the service law.

As to the law, it is to be found in the *Manual of Military Law, Manual of Air Force Law* etc., and in Queen's Regulations. They are in the law libraries and as already indicated, obtainable from HMSO, but far more often than not the law will be identical with what you already know and practise. Certainly I have never encountered the advocate who had any problem in finding and easily understanding the relevant law. The books are written with a view to their being understood by serving officers and they are an example to us all.

If you are lucky enough to be instructed in court martial work then enjoy it. There is no nicer way of practising the profession of advocate.

Postscript

There, then, is the small bag of tools to get you started. Small it certainly is, with far more left out than put in. During the writing of this book a lot of my colleagues were kind enough to read bits of it, and every one of them had something useful to add. If I had expanded the manuscript to include all the helpful points raised, it is certain the book would have been twice as long and may never even have been completed.

When the first edition came out, indeed, I was surprised and delighted to receive letters from, quite literally, all over the Commonwealth and the United States, many of which contained valuable suggestions. (The most far-flung, incidentally, came from a young solicitor working in the Solomon Islands. He had finished in court too late to catch the canoe — yes, *the canoe* — back to the island where the air-strip was, and he spent the night under a tin roof on a South Pacific beach, writing by the light of a hurricane lamp.) I kept a file of the comments and suggestions, adding to it over the next ten years and slowly developing a simplified system of 'rules' which I felt would make the learning of the skills of advocacy a much less difficult affair. My publishers brought these out under the title *The Golden Rules of Advocacy*, and if you have found any benefit from this Beginner's Guide, then you may enjoy the extra suggestions and somewhat different formulations set out in the *Golden Rules*.

But when it comes to rules, do remember that there are as many right ways of following the craft of advocacy as there are disciplined and imaginative minds. As was emphasised much earlier in this book, when you are thoroughly familiar with all the basic rules, don't be afraid to break them, and don't forget that it's the advocate who is willing to do it differently who stands out from the crowd. Apart from mandatory requirements, such as putting your case and laying your ground, there are few strict rules that cannot be handled with originality.

Keep looking for that original approach, for a better way of doing it. And if you think you have hit upon a new and useful piece of advice, a new formulation of how to do it better or of how to stay out of trouble, please don't keep it to yourself. Drop me a line, if you will, and share it with the rest of us. I can always be reached either *via* 1 Gray's Inn Square, London WC1, or *via* the California office of my American firm, Speiser Krause & Madole, Two Park Plaza, Suite 1060, Irvine, California 92714-5904.

Above all, when you feel afraid, when your mouth goes dry and you feel inadequate, remember that this has been the common experience of every one of us. You will find it gets easier, as we all did. Don't feel defeated by the failures that are out there waiting for you. Don't be overwhelmed by them when they arrive. When you feel at your very lowest, remember that we have all been there: we have all felt the same. It does get better and it goes on getting better. In the end it almost becomes an addiction: it certainly becomes a way of life.

Good luck.